CREATION or EVOLUTION

A Home-Study

Creation Curriculum

(Third Edition)

Presented by

MISSION: IMPERATIVE!

Written by Mike Snavely

What is *"Mission: Imperative!"*?

- *Some key elements of this ministry:*
    1. *The ministry exists to give God His rightful glory in creation. We are a 501(c)(3) not-for-profit organization founded in 1995, and operate under the authority of a board. We are financially supported by churches and individuals. The ministry was founded by Mike & Carrie Snavely (brief bio on page 147). Mike is the president and does the speaking.*
    2. *The ministry is mainly involved in presenting creation-oriented seminars in churches, camps, and other venues to which they are invited to present the gospel through the message of creation. There are eight sessions in the regular line-up, known as the "Seminar Safari" (there are other topics as well, several of which are more specialized, and new topics are developed from time to time). The ministry produces DVDs on a range of creation-oriented topics, and Mike has also written a curriculum and become involved in book writing. Furthermore, creation and flood-oriented "safaris" have been added to the ministry to give people a unique and close-up experience in these areas.*
    3. *The ministry is based in Jonestown, PA. Seminars are presented all over the USA and internationally.*

To book a seminar series, contact us at *www.natureofcreation.org*

Statement of Faith of
MISSION: IMPERATIVE!

- We believe that the Scriptures of the Old and the New Testaments are verbally inspired by God and inerrant in the original writings, and that they are the supreme and final authority in faith and life.
- We believe in one God, eternally existing in three equal yet distinct persons: Father, Son and Holy Spirit.
- We believe that Jesus Christ was begotten by the Holy Spirit, born of the Virgin Mary, and is true God and true man. We believe in the resurrection of the crucified body of our Lord from the dead, His ascension into Heaven and His present ministry on our behalf as mediator, advocate, and intercessor.
- We believe that the Holy Spirit is a person, and that He convicts, teaches, guides and empowers. We believe He gives gifts to Christians for the building up of the Church.
- We believe that man was created in the image of God, that he sinned, and thereby incurred not only physical death but also spiritual death, which is separation from God, and that all human beings are born with a sinful nature, and that they must be born again to be accepted by the Holy God.
- We believe that the Lord Jesus Christ died for our sins, according to the Scriptures, as a representative and substitutionary sacrifice, and that all who believe in Him are justified on the ground of His shed blood, and are saved by grace through faith wholly apart from human merit and works.
- We believe that all who receive the Lord Jesus Christ by faith are born again, indwelt by the Holy Spirit and thereby become children of God. We believe that they are also sealed by the Holy Spirit, thus being secured unto the day of redemption.
- We believe that Satan is a personal being, a fallen angel, the prince of demons, the great enticer and deceiver and that his destiny is eternal punishment.
- We believe that the Scriptures clearly teach that every believer should live a life set apart from all worldly and sinful practices, to abide in Christ and to walk in the Spirit.
- We believe that Jesus Christ will personally return to the earth to rule and reign.
- We believe in the bodily resurrection of every person, the saved to eternal blessedness and the unsaved to eternal punishment.
- Furthermore, we believe that the age of the earth can be measured in thousands, not millions, of years.

Contents

Instructions

It is important that you read these instructions before you start. They will help you to understand various aspects of the course.

- There are a total of thirty-eight lessons divided into seven units of study.
- There is a worksheet with the final "Conclusion" at the end of the last unit.
- Each lesson is designed to take 10 – 20 minutes to complete.
- You will notice several symbols on the pages of this curriculum. Here is a list of what they are and what they mean:

  - Do the practical work assignment that accompanies this symbol.

 - You might have to put on your "thinking cap" when you see this. There could be questions that have to be thought through.

 - Complete all reading and practical assignments up to this point before continuing any further with the lesson.

 - Lesson continues on the next page.

 - End of lesson.

 - We have produced a series of videos that can go hand-in-hand with this course. The videos are live seminar presentations of this material. If you have this series (available at www.natureofcreation.org), you can watch the appropriate video when you see this icon. The number above the icon is the number of the video you will watch at that point, before the test is taken.

Unit Test - End of unit – take the unit test before continuing to the next unit.

- You will find the tests and the test answer keys at the back of the book. These have been placed together there so that you can remove them conveniently before the student begins the course.
- Not all lessons have worksheets; most do. All units have tests at the end.

IMPORTANT:
TEACHER, PLEASE READ THESE TWO PAGES BEFORE STARTING!
(You need to know what is being discussed in this book.)

WHAT IS CREATION?

"To cause to come into existence; bring into being; make; originate; to make something requiring art, skill, invention, etc.; to bring about; give rise to" - (Webster's)

The Bible teaches that God created everything that is in the universe (space, earth and sea) and heaven. He started with nothing, and made everything. If creation meant that God brought order out of matter that was not in order, then that would mean that matter already existed. We would still be left with the question: "Where did the matter come from?" Biblical creation means that God spoke, and out of the power of His own being brought everything into existence and order. He did this for His own good pleasure.

The Bible is the source of information on creation. Nature verifies this creative genius. Evidence from nature verifies the biblical version (and ONLY the biblical version) of creation.

WHAT IS EVOLUTION?

"To develop by gradual changes; unfold; opening out, or working out; process of development, as from simple to complex form; gradual, progressive change; the development of a species, organism, or organ from its original or primitive state to its present or specialized state" - (Webster's)

Evolution, as it is used and understood by most people, claims that somehow all things originally came into being (whether God - or something supernatural - was involved, or all by natural, chance means), and then changed slowly over many years, becoming more and more complex. This is known as MACROEVOLUTION, or Darwinian evolution, or naturalism. Purely naturalistic evolution attempts to explain the existence of energy and matter without anything supernatural. This means that people who believe this idea claim that the universe, all galaxies and solar systems, our earth and everything on it, and all life were brought into being by random, chance, natural events over billions of years of time.

MICROEVOLUTION, on the other hand, is defined as minor genetic changes that are sometimes observed to take place (like feather colors, or tail length, etc.), but ALWAYS ONLY within a KIND of creature. Microevolution has nothing whatsoever in common with macroevolution (Darwinism).

Man, and the books he writes on the subject, is the source of information on evolution. Evolution theory constantly changes as new attempts to explain things by natural means replace outdated attempts to do the same.

WHAT IS "INTELLIGENT DESIGN"?

Perhaps this is a term you've heard before. Some people make the mistake of thinking that intelligent design (or ID) is the same thing as biblical creation. It's NOT! Here's why....

As you will see from the lessons in this book, Darwinian evolution is called a science theory. As such, it MUST be held to the rules of science. The basic rule of a science theory is that it must be testable. You have to be able to actually test a science theory in laboratory conditions to see if it works or not. Darwinian evolution, in all the details, has been tested for a very long time – over 150 years! To many (if not most) scientists, the tests show that this theory does NOT even come close to explaining either the origins of matter or living things on the earth, nor how they developed into <u>very complex</u> living things! Therefore, after becoming aware of these results, many scientists admit that evolution is not the answer. But, they're still left with the basic question: If not by evolution, then where did complex living things come from? Their answer is simply that there must have been an intelligent designer ...somehow ...somewhere!

Please note that intelligent design offers no information as to who or what the intelligent designer was or is, and how or when it happened. It is also not a science theory in and of itself, since there is nothing specific to test. There are certain aspects that can be tested, of course. For example, scientists have put together a formula for proving the existence of intelligence. These tests can certainly be done in laboratory conditions, but all they reveal is the presence of intelligence, and not who or what or when or how.

Biblical creation, however, is very specific. The Bible teaches that there was indeed a creation "in the beginning". Furthermore, it specifies who the designer is (Jesus) and it specifies when He did it, how long it took, and to a degree, how He did it. Creation is not a science theory because the act of creating is not available to be tested in laboratory conditions. Creation is a biblical assertion. Intelligent design only presents the conclusion that there was indeed a designer, but nothing else.

Intelligent design is a threat to evolution – especially in schools – not because it acknowledges Jesus as the Creator, but because it doesn't exclude the possibility that there MIGHT have been a deity involved in original design. Many evolutionists cannot tolerate that. They don't want to acknowledge the existence of God, or at least His involvement with man, especially on the sin issue. Therefore, many of them will loudly proclaim that those who want to teach ID in the classroom are trying to get "young earth creationism" into the schools. WRONG! Teaching ID in schools is simply being honest about the scientific problems related to evolution theory.

(By the way, many evolutionists do believe in God, claiming that He was somehow involved in the evolutionary process. This is false. God would never have used something so inefficient and painful as evolution to do His creating.)

UNIT 1

THE CREATION

Genesis 1 & 2

WHY STUDY GENESIS?

We're at the beginning of a direct study of the first eleven chapters of Genesis. It doesn't seem like very much material, but there's a lot of important information packed into those chapters. Our study won't cover all of the topics found there, but what we will look at is extremely important for understanding much of the rest of the Bible. The message of God's Word basically revolves around the themes of sin and salvation. This unit will cover just the first two chapters.

There are several reasons to study the book of Genesis. You might think of some of your own reasons why we should do this, but we list just three here:

1. To understand the world, past and present. In upcoming lessons, we will look at some very interesting ways in which the world was a very different place than it is today.

2. To recognize **COMPROMISE** when we see it. A good example of compromise would be when people accept part of what evolution teaches just so that others who don't believe the Bible won't laugh at them. We need to know and study the Bible so that when people teach wrong things about it, we can recognize their errors and not be led astray into false teachings.

3. To build back into our society the Godly values and principles that the Bible teaches. What do we mean by that? Well, if you plant an apple seed, what type of fruit are you going to eat from the tree that will grow? Pears? Plums? No, apples, of course! Look at the picture here to the right. It shows a tree. But, let's imagine that the seed is evolution. What do you think the "fruit" will be from a "seed" like that?

    If evolution is true, then there is NO MEANING to life. Life only has the meaning that YOU give it. You are born, you live, and then you die. There is no PURPOSE for you to be on earth, nor is there hope when you die. There's certainly CONFUSION. You're just an accident of nature.

If evolution is true, then there is no such thing as LAW. Who says that you can't steal if you want to? Who made up that law? Some government? Why can't you murder someone if you want to? Who made up the law that says you can't do that? After all, if evolution says that we got here through *survival of the fittest*, then what's wrong with trying to prove it?

If evolution is true, there's no such thing as RIGHT or WRONG. There's no MORALITY. Who said that you can't cheat? Why is it wrong to tell a lie? These things are just natural, right?

If evolution is true, there is no ORDER in life. Everything just happens by chance. If you do something against some law, it's not your fault. You couldn't help it! The desire to do the thing that you did was just accidentally passed down to you from your parents.

Now, if a society believes in evolution, it will begin to act like it. Evolution gives free reign – a free license – for people to sin by calling it "your nature". Do you see evidence of this in the world around you? What is the news filled with? Violence, perversions, drugs, suicide, robbery, etc. Ask yourself a question: Should any of these things come as a surprise to us? No, they shouldn't! Yes, these things are terrible, but they are just the natural results of sin and the teachings of "naturalism".

But, let's now look at the creation side:

If you were created, that makes a huge difference in your outlook on life. There is MEANING to life. God does not make mistakes. You are special, made in His image. You're not an accident…there is a specific PURPOSE for your existence. God loves *you*!

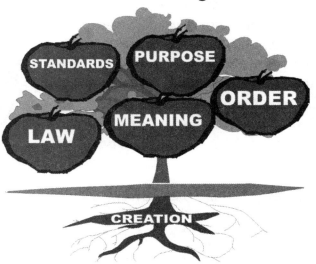

If you were created, there are LAWS to live by; not man-made laws, but God's laws for life. There are moral STANDARDS that God put in place. Many people think that if they become Christians, God wants to take away all of their

Do you enjoy sports? Any game is governed by its rules. In football, what if the referee never blew his whistle? What if the players on the field could do whatever they wanted to do? Would you enjoy the game? No, you'd get bored very quickly. *The game only has meaning because of the rules, and if they are obeyed.* It's the same with the "rules of life" that God has given. Life only has true meaning & enjoyment if it's lived according to *His* rules.

"fun" by requiring that they follow His laws. This is not true! God's laws are there to *protect* us. He knows how we work since He made us. He knows what will get us into trouble, so He made laws to protect us from harm and to keep peace among men. Besides, God is the one who created "fun", too.

God also created NATURAL LAW. These are the laws by which nature functions. These laws control things like gravity and light. If God did not make these things, and set laws by which they work, how did they come into existence, and how do they work so perfectly? Evolution can neither explain their existence, nor why they work like they do.

If you were created, there is ORDER. God is the one who placed the stars into beautiful galaxies. God is the one who created color. God is the one who created the weather systems that water the earth. God is the one who made certain atoms to form into molecules so that we have something we can use (example: two atoms of hydrogen and one atom of oxygen can chemically bond to make one, tiny molecule of water. Many millions of these molecules put together give us a tiny drop of water!). God is the one who made the laws that keep our solar system together. God is the one who made male and female (evolution CANNOT explain this!). God invented marriage. In every way, and in every living thing, God created order. Without it, there would be total chaos.

As you can see, what you believe about origins is extremely important. The teachings of evolution have replaced the truth with a lie, they have removed God's rightful glory and credit in His creation, they serve to remove God's blessing, and they have created much doubt in God's Word.

If we remove God from our minds as our Creator, it becomes a simple matter to remove Him from our minds as our Savior as well.

THE CREATION

A quick look at the issue....

*I*f you were to look at a car parked in a lot, would you conclude that dust, chemicals, water, heat, cold, time, chance, etc. created the car? Of course not. You know that the car first had a designer, then somebody else built the car following the design. The car can't build itself all by accident from mud and chemicals.

Why, then, would people conclude that these types of accidents produced the universe and everything in it, including living things? It very quickly becomes a question of how people could possibly be so "blind" to believe that. This is not just a science issue – this is a spiritual issue. The Bible refers to this kind of blindness in several places (for examples, see II Thessalonians 2:10-12; II Corinthians 4:3-4). Many people refuse to accept the Bible as God's Word and what it teaches. These passages in the Bible infer that, because they refused to accept the truth, these people have been blinded by the "god of this world" (Satan) so that they CANNOT believe the truth.

So, where did all these creatures come from, then? Did it rain one day on some mud, and...well, out came a butterfly eventually? Did lightning strike some muddy water long ago and accidentally start making a zebra? Did they make themselves? No. Someone designed and built them.

Most people believe that there are only two possible explanations for the existence of all things. Either they made themselves by pure chance through the very long process called EVOLUTION, or everything was made by God through CREATION. In the coming lessons, we'll look at both ideas.

First, to Genesis....

CREATION *is God's idea.* EVOLUTION *is man's idea. So, we'll look at what God says that He did, and then we'll look at what man says happened.*

Let's start by looking at what God says. In order to do that, we need to look into the first book of the Bible, GENESIS. The word Genesis means "beginnings" or "origins". The first eleven chapters of Genesis contain much of the information we need to know about the origins of many things on Earth. We can divide these eleven chapters into five basic ideas, or topics. Dividing up these chapters in this way makes it easier to study the different events. The chart below shows us the five main topics.

TOPIC	CHAPTER
1. The Creation	Chapters 1 & 2
2. The Fall of Man	Chapter 3
3. The Patriarchs	Chapters 4, 5, 10 & 11
4. The Flood	Chapters 6, 7, 8, & 9
5. The Nations	Chapter 11

✱ *Read Chapter 1 of Genesis, then answer the following questions:*

1. How long did God take to create everything? _____

2. On the third day, what did God do to the water? _____

_____

3. On which day did God make plants? _____

4. On which day did God make birds? _____

5. On which day did God make "creeping creatures"? _____

6. **THINK!** On which day did God make dinosaurs? _____

7. When He was finished, what did God say about His work? _____

8. **THINK!** What was the first thing God made in our universe? _____

9. What did God make on the fourth day? _____

10. What was the difference between man's food and the animals' food? _____

_____

DAY #SIX

It's amazing to have a brief look at the events of creation. The written account sure is brief. God doesn't go into detail to tell us all about how He made each flower, each plant or tree, or each creature. He doesn't tell us why He made each thing the way He did. The bulk of the creation account is covered in just one chapter – just 31 verses.

From Genesis chapter one, it is clear that God does things so differently than we do. If we want to do a good job on a project on which we're working, it takes us a long time to plan it out and then do the actual work. Even then, it's not perfect. But God just SPOKE, and things came into being!! God formed other things from dust. And, everything was perfect, too. God said that all of the things He made were good.

In Genesis chapter one, we read about God's creation of everything right up to the first man and woman, whom He created last. But, let's pause a moment to consider how perfect this needed to be. Let's consider a few amazing facts:

1. Light was made on the first day. But the sun was not made until the fourth day. Why? And, what was the source of the light for the first three days? It's very clear from the Genesis account of creation that the sun is an ARTIFICIAL source of light. That means that it produces light, but light and energy exist apart from it – just like a candle or flashlight. God evidently lit the earth by some other way for the first three days. Why did He do this? We don't know, but perhaps He did it knowing that one day man would try to explain things by evolution. Evolution requires that the sun be there FIRST before anything else could evolve.

   Here's another interesting fact: Scientists do not even know what light is!

2. The trees and plants were all made on the third day of creation (evolution requires that life began in the oceans). If these creation days were millions of years, what pollinated all the flowering plants until bees and butterflies were made on the sixth day? Clearly, from this example alone, the days of creation were literal single rotations of the earth. Flowering plants could easily survive for three days before being pollinated.

3. "Nothing works until everything works". This is a very true statement when it comes to living things. There is absolutely no way that any living organism could survive without all of its basic bodily organs and functions perfectly in place, fully complex, and operating right from the start. But, this is also true with all of the aspects of the creation. Everything must be perfectly in place before ANYTHING can work.

   Nyah! Nyah! We were first!

4. Note that birds were made BEFORE any land animals. Why? Again, we don't know. God doesn't tell us, but perhaps the same "evolution stumbling block" applies here, too. Evolution requires that reptiles (which were made on the sixth day) come before birds.

Genesis chapter two is not a different account of creation, as some people have thought. Chapter two focuses in on the main events of the sixth day of creation. It expands it a bit more for us and gives more details of what went on during that day. Let's see what it has to say...

✱ Read Chapter 2 of Genesis, then answer the following questions:

1. From what did God form Adam? _____

2. How was the ground watered? _____

3. Where did God put Adam? _____

4. What two trees stood in the middle of the Garden? _____

   _____

5. What were the names of the four headwaters at Eden? _____

   _____

6. What was Adam's work? _____

7. From what tree was Adam *NOT* allowed to eat? _____

8. **THINK!** Did Adam name *ALL* the creatures? _____

9. Which ones did he name? _____

   _____

10. What was not found among the creatures that God brought to Adam? _____

    _____

11. From what did God make Eve? _____

12. Why was Eve called "woman"? _____

    _____

HOW LONG WAS A CREATION "DAY"?

When you read Genesis chapter one, how many days does it say God took to create everything? Six, right? Then He rested on the seventh day. But, over the years there have been many people who tell us that the days of creation were not really days at all, but millions, or even billions of years. Why would they say that? Could the word "day" mean something other than a 24-hour period, as we understand it? Actually, yes it can. The Old Testament was written in Hebrew, and the word in Hebrew for "day" can mean a 24-hour rotation of the earth, or it can mean "daylight", or it can mean an "indefinite period of time". So, what does it mean in this passage? How much time was involved in "the six days of creation"? We need to answer this question because it's actually an important issue. Here's the answer:

A "day" in chapter one is a 24-hour rotation of the earth.

How do we know this? We'll look at that in a moment, but first, let's understand why some people believe that the days were billions of years. It all started over a hundred and fifty years ago when a man by the name of Charles Darwin, pictured at left, wrote a book called Origin of Species. This book convinced many people that the theory (the idea) of evolution was true. His book became very famous, and soon, even many scientists began believing in evolution. But could they see evolution actually happening? Could they see one type of creature turning into another type? Could they see animals make themselves all by chance? Could they see any evidence, maybe from fossils, that this had been occurring in the past? No, they couldn't, so they said that all these changes in animals must have taken place very slowly – VERY slowly. So slowly, in fact, that it could NEVER be seen. So, they were forced to say that these slow, evolutionary changes took place over many millions of years. Therefore, huge amounts of time were needed if the theory of evolution stood a chance of being believable.

The idea became so popular, that even some church leaders began to believe it. They thought that science had proved evolution because that's what they were told. Furthermore, if they believed evolution was true, they had to believe that the earth was billions of years old, too. But, that made a big problem for them, because they also believed the Bible. The Bible teaches that the earth is MUCH younger than the evolutionists say it is, so these Christians began to try to interpret the Bible by what the scientists were saying. **BIG MISTAKE!!** Christians should NEVER choose science over the Bible! Besides, scientists are sometimes wrong.

Anyway, some of these Christians began to look in the Bible to see where these millions of years might fit in. Various ideas were proposed. One group believed they found the answer. They said that the "days" of creation must not be literal days after all, but "ages" of time. Therefore, they believed, the six days were actually millions, or even billions, of years. But, as we'll now see, this is not what the Bible teaches.

*Many people now believe that the world is billions of years old. Some Christians don't want to appear foolish or ignorant, so they say they believe it, too. Others believe it simply because they really don't know the truth. They just accept it because it's what they're taught. Still other Christians believe the idea that science can explain the miraculous events of the creation week, and "science" now says the earth is billions of years old. However, a miracle is not explainable, and creation is a miracle. It falls outside of what science can explain. A miracle is always both instant and perfect. It seems that often when a miracle cannot be explained scientifically, the closest scientific explanation is accepted instead of what the Bible plainly teaches. So, look at the chart below. It will show that, according to the Bible, day #6 was not a million-year period, and if **it** wasn't, neither were the others.*

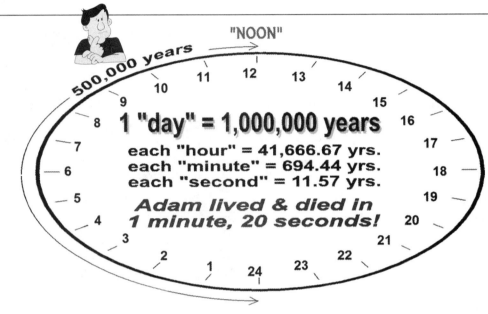

Some people believe that there were too many events on creation day #6 for it to have been just a 24-hour day. They think that it had to be *much* longer than that. Therefore, let's imagine that this day was 1 million years. Now, when we consider all that God made during that day, let's say that God made Adam later in the day, perhaps at "noon", right in the middle of the whole time period. Therefore, during the "morning" (500,000 years) God made all the land animals, and then Adam at noon. Then, in the "afternoon" He moved Adam to the Garden of Eden and gave him instructions. Then, Adam named the animals that God brought to him and having completed this job, God put him to sleep and created Eve. These are the events of day #6. Now, if day #6 was a million years, and if we divide the million-year "day" into 24 equal periods (just like a day has 24 equal hours), the problems become clear. The Bible states that Adam lived 930 years. If so, then he would have died 1 minute and 20 seconds after he was made! (If he was made at noon, then he would have died at 12:01:20pm!) *However*, the Bible states that sin entered the world through Adam, so if Adam was made and lived and died on day #6, that would mean that sin entered the world on day #6, right? But that can't be, because according to Genesis 1:31, as the sixth day closes, everything is still "very good"! Sin cannot be considered "very good", so the only logical conclusion is that it couldn't possibly have been a long time period. It was a literal, 24-hour day. If we insist on a long period, then we'd also have to conclude that the Bible is wrong in certain areas -- that Adam didn't live 930 years, or that he didn't sin, or that the sixth day did not end "very good", etc.

This is further made plain for us in Exodus 20:8-11 where God makes the clear statement that the Jewish people are to work for **six days and rest on the seventh**. Why? Because God says that He himself laid the pattern down by doing exactly that when He created the world.

Also, if the writer of Genesis, Moses, had really meant to give us the idea that these creation days were very long periods of time, there are other Hebrew words he could have used that would have been much clearer. Why didn't he use them?

Furthermore, in Matthew 19:4, Jesus himself says that "in the beginning" the Creator made them male and female, referring here to people. Notice that He used the same words that the Bible begins with. He was referring to the six creation days. BUT....since there are only about 6,000 years since Adam was made, Jesus more likely would have referred to the creation of humans as being MUCH more recent if "in the beginning" meant millions of years ago.

Remember that the Bible is the only book that you can trust without question!

Now that you have read, in these two chapters, the creation account of the origins of everything, it's interesting to note that not everything is covered in detail. There are some things we can perhaps make a fairly good guess about what God did, even though the verses might not be specific. For example, there was probably only one big continent on Earth at the beginning. How do we know that? Because verse nine of Genesis chapter one says that the water was "gathered together unto <u>one</u> place". That all changed at the time of the flood (Genesis 6-8). We'll cover that later.

Another area we can make a pretty good guess about is that there was possibly no rain from the creation right up to the time of the flood. That's 1,656 years! Verses five and six of Genesis chapter two give us a pretty good head start on this idea.

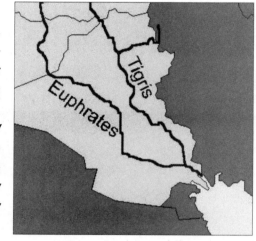

Now, think about this! Look at the map to the right. It's a view of two rivers found mainly in the modern-day country of Iraq. This area is also known as "Greater Mesopotamia". Mesopotamia means "between the rivers". The two rivers are the Tigris and the Euphrates. Many people think that the Garden of Eden was located somewhere in this area. They naturally get that idea from Genesis 2:14, which mentions these names. But, in Genesis 2:10-14 we learn that there is only ONE river at Eden, and we are not told its name. However, the Tigris (Hiddekel) and Euphrates are mentioned with two others, not as major rivers, though, but as "heads". A head or headwater is part of the source of a larger river. The modern Tigris and Euphrates are not headwaters – they're major rivers. The other two "heads" were called Pishon and Gihon. So, according to many biblical scholars, the modern rivers (which probably started flowing after the great flood of Noah's time) were just named by people who discovered them after the flood as they moved there from the area where Noah's ark settled. They used names they perhaps had a record of since before the flood happened. Therefore, it is impossible to know where the Garden of Eden was originally located. The flood changed everything.

We'll discover other amazing things as we look further into the subject of origins. We will see that the earth was very different in the past in many different ways. Here are some of those ways:

- Man could live longer in the past compared to today - <u>MUCH</u> longer.
- The earth looked different. (Remember? There was probably just one continent.)
- There were some weird creatures in the past. Creatures like....dinosaurs!
- All people were vegetarians (they didn't eat meat); so were ALL creatures.
- There were no weather patterns like today. No tornados or hurricanes. No freezing winters and baking hot summers.
- People spoke only one language – all over the world!

To understand these events, we need to study the whole CREATION MODEL (see Pg. 45), not just the events recorded during the "Creation Week" (Genesis chapters 1 & 2). The CREATION MODEL, which is a term used to help us understand the whole picture of why things are the way they are today, is best understood by studying Genesis chapters 1–12, which includes the account of the flood. The flood is a major part of the whole CREATION MODEL.

Man's views of the world, and its beginnings, are often very different from what God says. Many people don't want to believe what God says in His Word, so they invent things to believe in. Then, they often teach these false ideas to others through books, in movies, on TV, in schools, and through other means. Eventually, people begin to believe these made-up stories. One of the false stories is the idea called EVOLUTION. Evolution is a man-made story about where everything in the universe came from. It tries to explain where everything came from without God doing it. Evolution says that everything just made itself all by natural, random, chance events.

People who believe in evolution have a LOT of explaining to do. For example, why is there male AND female? Why are there different languages? Why do we wear clothing? (animals don't). Where did music come from? Why are there seven days in a week? Who invented marriage?

Evolution has no explanation for many, many puzzlers like this. But, the Bible answers many of these basic questions. Let's find out the origins of some of them that are found in the first two chapters of Genesis by playing a matching game.

✳ Look up the verses on the left. Draw a line to the matching event on the right.

1. Genesis 1:1	Origin of man
2. Genesis 1:9	Origin of the need for a man to marry
3. Genesis 1:11	Origin of the earth
4. Genesis 1:20	Origin of vegetation and trees
5. Genesis 1:27	Origin of marriage
6. Genesis 1:31	Origin of dry ground
7. Genesis 2:15	Origin of woman
8. Genesis 2:18	Origin of sea creatures and birds
9. Genesis 2:22	Origin of man working
10. Genesis 2:24	Everything was perfect at the beginning

Up to this point in the Bible, everything is fantastic. Creation is finished just the way God wanted it. It's perfect! But, as we're about to see, events now take a drastic turn for the worse.....

UNIT 2

THE FALL OF MAN

&

THE BEGINNING

OF NATIONS

Genesis 3 – 5, 10 & 11

THE FALL OF MAN

Missing the mark

*C*hapter three of the book of Genesis introduces us to a subject that is found throughout the rest of the Bible - SIN. Sin is one of the central themes in the Bible because it is man's basic problem. Sin is "missing the mark". God wants us to be perfect, but we certainly miss that mark, don't we? Adam was told, in Genesis chapter two, not to eat from the "tree of the knowledge of good and evil". Adam missed that mark, and in so doing, sinned.

At the beginning, God and man had a wonderful relationship. Everything was beautiful until Adam disobeyed. This sin caused a separation from God that has been passed on down to everybody ever since. Let's take a few minutes and read about this terrible event, and what it caused. Remember: this is a study on ORIGINS. As you read the passage, think about the things that are just beginning. Think about what is happening for the first time.

✳ *Read Chapter 3 of Genesis, then answer these questions:*

In these verses, either something is happening for the first time, or we can see the origin of something. Circle the letter of the correct answer.

1. verses 1 – 5

    a. The creation of snakes.
    b. The *tactics* of Satan.
    c. The woman sinning.
    d. A serpent learning to speak.

2. verse 6

    a. An apple being eaten.
    b. Gathering fruit.
    c. Giving in to temptation - SIN.
    d. Killing a deadly snake.

3. verse 7

    a. The making of the first clothing.
    b. Adam & Eve awoke from sleep.
    c. Fig leaves being eaten.
    d. People sewing animal skins.

4. verses 14 & 15

    a. Eve kills the snake.
    b. The serpent becomes wild.
    c. The serpent crawls on its belly.
    d. The snake strikes Adam.

5. verse 16

    a. A woman becomes pregnant.
    b. A woman wants to be married.
    c. Women will have pain in childbirth.
    d. A man becomes king.

6. verse 17

    a. Man begins to eat dirt.
    b. Man begins to curse the ground.
    c. Man listens to woman.
    d. Man begins "painful" farming.

7. verse 18 & 19

    a. Thorns & thistles emerge.
    b. Man begins eating thorns & thistles.
    c. Man begins to eat meat.
    d. Man sweats while eating.

8. verse 21

    a. People make clothing from skin.
    b. An animal dies.
    c. People improve their fig clothing.
    d. People discard their clothing.

SIN'S PENALTY & PAYMENT

So, what does all this mean?

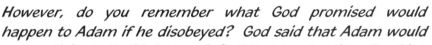

So far we've seen that, according to the Bible, everything was perfect at the beginning because that's just the way God does things. We've seen that Adam and Eve, the first man and woman, could eat from any plants in the garden where they lived – all except one. We've seen that they were tempted to disobey. They yielded to that temptation and sinned. With that sin came certain punishments. One of those punishments was that Adam would now have a hard life working the soil to provide food for his family.

However, do you remember what God promised would happen to Adam if he disobeyed? God said that Adam would surely die! Well, did Adam die? Of course he did. The Bible tells us so in Genesis 5:5. However,

his sin brought much more serious consequences than just his death. The Bible goes on to tell us that the whole creation was cursed because of Adam's sin. Worse yet, the curse of his sin was passed down to all his descendants. Guess what! That means YOU and ME! We are ALL born "in Adam". That means we are all going to suffer the same fate as Adam.

But, his death was not just physical. By that we mean that it wasn't just the body that dies, but this death is also spiritual – the REAL person living inside the body is condemned. This is very bad news for all humans! The Bible teaches us that we are LOST because of our sin. We are all born into Adam's family, so we're all sinners. The Bible states that because God is a holy and just God, He cannot allow sin in His presence. Therefore, when we die, we cannot go to God. We will be sent to the place called "hell" that has been prepared for Satan and his demons – forever! And, the Bible also teaches us that there is NOTHING you or I can do to get to heaven, where God is, when we die. There is no way we can pay the debt we owe to God to pay for our sin. As far as humans are concerned, it's hopeless for us! That is the bad news.

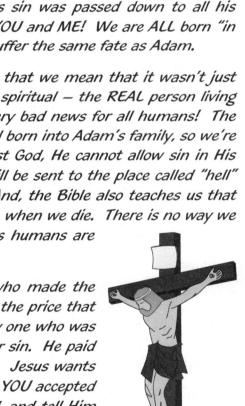

Now, here is the good news! Jesus Christ, the Son of God, who made the whole world, came down to Earth in the form of man, and paid the price that God demands to forgive people for their sins. Jesus was the only one who was perfect, and God accepted His death on the cross as payment for sin. He paid YOUR penalty and mine. It is a FREE gift that you cannot earn. Jesus wants each person to accept Him as his personal savior from sin. Have YOU accepted Him? All you have to do is believe that Jesus is the son of God, and tell Him that you are a sinner (He already knows it anyway). Tell Him that you are sorry for this, and that you accept his payment for you personally. Invite Him into your heart and life. Thank Him for saving you and giving you life everlasting. Your body will die (thanks, Adam!), but your spirit will live with Jesus forever! (Thank you, Jesus!)

But, don't take our word for it. Let's see what God Himself has to say…

The book of Romans, in the New Testament, spells this out pretty clearly for us. A few other places add insight to that. Let's look at a few verses found there that teach us what God wants us to know about His plan of salvation.

✳ *Read each of these verses, and then answer the questions:*

1. Romans 3:23

   Who has sinned? _____

   Of what have people fallen short? _____

2. Romans 6:23

   What are the wages of sin? That is, what is the payment, or penalty, of sin? _____

   What is the gift of God? _____

   Through whom does this gift come? _____

3. Romans 5:8

   Who loves us? _____

   How did He show this love? _____

4. Romans 10:9 and 13

   Who can call on the name of the Lord Jesus? _____

   What must you confess? _____

   What must you sincerely believe in your heart? _____

   Having done this, what will happen? _____

5. Ephesians 2:8-9

   To be saved from sin is a gift from God. Can you work for this gift? _____

   How do you receive this gift? _____

   What can't you boast about? _____

6. John 3:16

   People who believe in God's only son will not what? _____

"Neither is there salvation in any other; for there is no other name under heaven given among men, whereby we must be saved." – Acts 4:12 (KJV)

16

So, how is Jesus' death related to Genesis?

Jesus himself knew that Genesis was an accurate and true historical book. He referred to it more than to any other Old Testament book. Why? You see, if the events in Genesis are not true, then there would have been no need for Jesus to have gone to the cross. Genesis tells us where sin came from. Genesis tells us who did it. Genesis tells us where it happened. Genesis tells us who made everything. Genesis tells us how long it took. Genesis tells us many other things, too. If a person says that one of these events is untrue or inaccurate, how does that person know if any of the other events in the Bible are inaccurate, too? If one event is false, why aren't they all false? You see, you either believe the whole thing, or you don't. The Bible is VERY clear about these things! This is why the issue about how long the days of creation were is so important.

Let's return to the length of the creation days for a moment...

The Bible makes it very clear, from the evidence we've seen in an earlier lesson, that He created in six, literal days. If a person looks at this and says, "Well, I know the Bible SAYS six days, but that's not REALLY what it means", then that same person, using that same reasoning, could look at the words of Jesus and say, "Yes, I know Jesus SAID that you must be born again, but that's not REALLY what He meant".

Do you see the danger there? Where would that kind of reasoning stop? How would you know which portions of the Bible are true, and which are not? If we say we believe the Bible, doesn't it make sense to accept what it says as truth? After all, the Bible is God's Word and declares itself to be truth (John 17:17). God created everything. Don't you think that He knows how long it took? Let's accept what He says as truth, even if we don't understand all of it.

THE PATRIARCHS (PART 1)

*W*hat in the world is a PATRIARCH? A patriarch is a father or leader of a family or tribe. In many cases, the patriarch is the founder of a family or colony, and is usually looked up to with reverence. In this lesson, we move away from the Garden of Eden, from which Adam and Eve have been banished. You will now meet their children, grandchildren, great-grandchildren, great, great-grandchildren, etc. Some of these people were very honorable, while others....well, some weren't so honorable. Some accomplished amazing things while others seem to just disappear into history. Let's meet the first two, Cain and Abel.

✱ *Read Chapter 4 of Genesis, then answer this question:*

How many "firsts" or origins can you find in this passage? Write them down here with the verse where you found it.

(example)   murder - verse 8

_____   _____

_____   _____

_____   _____

*E*volutionists have had to use their imaginations to try to explain where things came from. But, what about things that people <u>do</u>, let alone where they came from? For example, where did music get its start? Who developed stringed instruments? Was it some sort of accident involving one of your "ancestors" tripping over a vine or something else that was stretched tightly? Who figured out that you could dig metals out of the ground and work with them? Who figured out that metal must be heated to turn it into something useful? Who invented art? And, why?

O-o-o-o! Heem mak wikka rokkim rollie!

"TOING"

As you've seen from the passage you just read, mankind was doing these things <u>right from the start.</u>

And, not only were they making metal objects and playing musical instruments, they were already instructing others how to do it, too! That's the opposite of what we expect from evolution. If man began as an ape-like creature, how did arts, crafts, music, etc. begin? How and why did an ape learn to make and appreciate a painting?

This chart at the right will give you a bit of an idea of what we're talking about. The first line, the vertical one, marks the beginning of time. Now, look at the "evolution model". At the beginning of time, man was a simple, primitive creature, but has gotten better and better as time has gone on. But, look at the "creation model". According to the Bible, it was just the exact opposite. Man started off being perfect. After all, the Bible says that God made man in His image and after He was finished, He called His work "very good". For

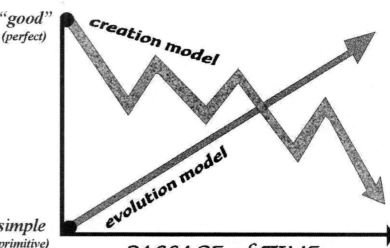

something to be very good in God's eyes would make it perfect! So, according to the Bible, man was made perfectly right in the beginning and was able to accomplish great things. His mind was perfect, and so was his body. There were no genetic flaws.

But, as you know, man sinned and brought about a curse. That has caused man to DEVOLVE (the opposite of evolution) ever since. Things have been getting worse, instead of better. They've become less complex, instead of more complex, even though great civilizations have risen and fallen.

This can be observed, too. It happens with everything we see. It happens with our bodies — we get old and weak. It happens with our houses — they crack and break, they need constant repair, and if you never do anything to them, they eventually fall down and rot. It happens with our cars — they get rusty and need lots of attention, so we eventually have to junk them. It's happening to the earth — it's spinning, but is slowing down. It happens to our languages — specialists have told us that all languages are getting simpler, and so is speech. It happens with everything we see. Everywhere we look, things are breaking down and getting less complex as time goes on. THE OPPOSITE HAS NEVER BEEN OBSERVED. But, the opposite is what evolution is completely based on!

> Most noble friends, have we not accomplished this honorable deed, to have justly wrought our task...

> Me an' my friends done good in school so, it's like...I'm gonna go chill out, dude. We ain't gonna....Wo! Like, wow! Check out them chicks! Them are, like, cool, man!

Great civilizations of the past have accomplished amazing things – quite the opposite of the evolution "ape-man" theory.

19

THE PATRIARCHS (PART 2)

*N*ow that you've read chapter 4 of Genesis, you've met some interesting people — people like Cain, Abel, Jabal, Jubal and Tubal-Cain. They all represent major "firsts" in history. Now, things begin to unfold rather rapidly. Adam's children have had children and grandchildren, and people begin to multiply. Chapters five, ten and eleven take us from Adam the whole way down to Noah (who built the ark) and on to Abram (later to be called Abraham). Basically, those chapters just give us lists of names and who was the father of whom.

But, there are some very interesting people along the way, and we'll stop and take a look at some of them on our journey through time.

Cain – the first murderer

In this next part of the lesson, we're going to read about these men. These chapters sort-of skip around a bit with the information, so we're going to do it in a way that makes it easier to follow.

❋ *Read Chapter 5 of Genesis, then skip to chapter 11, and read from verse 10 to the end of the chapter.*

What you've just read is a "straight through" account of all of the patriarchs from Adam to Abram. (There's one more chapter in Genesis that we haven't looked at yet, but we're going to save it for a later lesson. It's chapter 10, which covers the three sons of Noah. It gives us an account of these three patriarchs, but they fit in after the flood, so we will look at these men and their descendants at the end of the lessons where the flood is covered.)

Why do you suppose the Bible gives us this information on the patriarchs? After all, who would have considered this important? The answer lies mainly with Jewish tradition. Keeping records like this has always been very important to the Jews. And, it certainly helps us today to be able to piece history together with accurate records that go right back to the very beginning.

Notice, too, that the only names given here are those involved in the direct lineage from Adam to Noah, then Noah to Abram (the "father of the Jews"). Others who were alive during all those years are not considered as important — the names included in the list show that the Jewish nation has a direct link back to God and creation.

Even today, there are many people who enjoy studying their own genealogy, or family history. It gives us a good sense of who we are and where we came from. It's interesting to see who our ancestors were and what life was like for them where they lived, and when they lived on the earth.

Many of your own ancestors are mentioned in the Bible, too. Remember that from Noah came all of the people in the world today. All the patriarchs in his lineage listed before him are your direct ancestors, too! The simple exercise to follow includes a bit of information about some of them.

B	M	O	S	E	T	H	D	E	M
P	E	L	E	G	Q	O	V	C	H
J	T	U	A	X	R	E	D	W	F
U	H	D	J	M	B	N	O	A	H
B	U	O	I	A	E	O	Z	Y	A
A	S	N	I	P	P	C	C	S	M
L	E	G	A	C	V	H	H	L	F
E	L	N	D	H	A	B	E	L	I
H	A	B	A	K	L	I	R	T	T
S	H	E	M	W	R	B	N	G	H

Genesis Name Search

Below is a group of 15 names found in the book of Genesis. In fact, these names are found in the first eleven chapters of that book, and they are the most interesting people who lived in the first 2000 years of the history of our Earth.

The names are listed chronologically (in the order they appear in Genesis) and there are a few interesting facts about each person.

OBJECT: Find all 15 names in the box at left and circle each one.

HINT: The names run down, across, or at an angle. Also, letters might be used more than once. *Happy hunting!* (See if you can find these people in Genesis!)

Do you know who these people are?

ADAM - He was the first man and the first father. He named the animals that God brought to him. Through him, sin entered the world.

EVE - She was the first woman, the first mother, and was created from a rib taken from her husband, Adam, and was his helper. The serpent deceived her in Eden.

CAIN - He was the first son of Adam & Eve. He killed his brother, Abel.

ABEL - He was the second son of Adam & Eve. He brought a sacrifice to God that was acceptable, and was killed by his brother, Cain.

LAMECH - He was a descendant of Cain and had three interesting sons: Jabal, who became the father of those who raise livestock and live in tents (nomads); Jubal (listed next); and Tubal-cain, who forged all kinds of tools out of bronze & iron.

JUBAL - He was a son of Lamech and became the father of all who play the harp & flute.

SETH - He was another son of Adam & Eve. He replaced Abel.

ENOCH - He was the father of Methuselah. Enoch "walked with God; then he was no more, because God took him away."

METHUSELAH - He was the oldest man who ever lived (969 years). He was Noah's grandfather. Many scholars believe his name means "when he dies, judgment comes", and that proved true, because immediately following his death, the great flood came.

NOAH - He was righteous among the people of his time. He built the ark and survived the great flood along with his family and the "floating zoo".

SHEM - He was a son of Noah and survived the great flood on the ark.

HAM - He was another son of Noah and also survived the great flood on board the ark. He was cursed by his father following the flood.

JAPHETH - He was another son of Noah who survived the great flood on board the ark.

NIMROD - He was a grandson of Ham and was a mighty warrior and hunter. He founded the city of Babylon.

PELEG - In Peleg's time (at his birth) the earth was divided. This is believed by many biblical scholars to be the time that the present-day continents were born, possibly as a result of the oceans rising and covering the low-lying regions.

Genesis 5	GENESIS 10	GENESIS 11	I CHRONICLES 1	MATTHEW 1	LUKE 3
Adam					Adam
Seth					Seth
Enosh					Enosh
Kenan					Kenan
Mahalalel					Mahalalel
Jared					Jared
Enoch					Enoch
Methuselah					Methuselah
Lamech					Lamech
Noah	Noah	Noah	Noah		Noah
	Shem	Shem	Shem		Shem
	Arphaxad	Arphaxad	Arphaxad		Arphaxad
					Cainan
	Shelah	Shelah	Shelah		Shelah
	Eber	Eber	Eber		Eber
	Peleg	Peleg	Peleg		Peleg
		Reu	Reu		Reu
		Serug	Serug		Serug
		Nahor	Nahor		Nahor
		Terah	Terah		Terah
		Abraham	Abraham	Abraham	Abraham
				Isaac	Isaac
				Jacob	Jacob
				Judah	Judah
				Perez	Perez
				Hezron	Hezron
				Ram	Ram
				Amminadab	Amminadab
				Nahshon	Nahshon
				Salmon	Salmon
				Boaz	Boaz
				Obed	Obed
				Jesse	Jesse
				David	David
					Nathan
				Solomon	Mattatha
				Rehoboam	Menna
					Melea
				Abijah	Eliakim
				Asa	Jonam
					Joseph
				Jehoshaphat	Judah
				Jehoram	Simeon
					Levi
				Uzziah	Matthat
				Jotham	Jorim
				Ahaz	Eliezer
					Joshua
				Hezekiah	Er
				Manasseh	Elmadam
					Cosam
				Amon	Addi
				Josiah	Melki
				Jeconiah	Neri
					Shealtiel
				Shealtiel	
				Zerubbabel	Zerubbabel
					Rhesa
				Abiud	Joanan
					Joda
				Eliakim	Josech
					Semein
				Azor	Mattathias
					Maath
				Zadok	Naggai
					Esli
				Akim	Nahum
					Amos
				Eliud	Mattathias
					Joseph
				Eleazar	Jannai
					Melki
				Matthan	Levi
					Matthat
				Jacob	Heli
				Joseph	Joseph
				Jesus	Jesus

The 6 Genealogies

On this page are the 6 major genealogies found in the Bible. As you can see, three of them begin with Noah while one ends with him. Two of the accounts list the names from Adam to Noah. The period from Adam to Abraham is the key time for the whole "creation model".

THE PATRIARCHS (PART 3)

Now that you've read chapter 5 and the last half of chapter 11, do you see why we did it this way? It's so that you could read straight through from Adam to Abram. Do you know how many years it was from Adam to Noah? Or from Noah to Abram? The Bible tells us, but we have to add up all the ages of each of the men along the way to find out. Below is an interesting chart. It lists all the patriarchs and other men in the whole lineage from Adam down to Joseph (Abraham's great-grandson).

Here's how the chart works: Look at the black bar at the top. It has numbers there that are multiples of 100. Those are years, starting from creation at the left. Below the black line, you can see the names of all the men listed in the first eleven chapters of Genesis. First, find Adam. You can see that he starts at creation, then goes for 930 years. You can look up any other man and see more or less when he was born and when he died, and you can see each person's age when they died — it's the number at the end of his bar line.

This is very useful because it gives us a "picture" of a very interesting time in our Earth's history. There are two things we want to specifically notice about this chart now. First, notice when the flood of Noah's time takes place — 1656 years after creation. Then, notice how long mankind could live before the flood. Most lived over 900 years! Notice, too, how the life spans begin to drop after the flood. Why was this so? The flood caused big changes, not only to the earth, but it also reduced mankind to just eight people! This severely limited mankind's ability to pass down to the next generations GENETIC information (the code of life) that allowed man to live long.

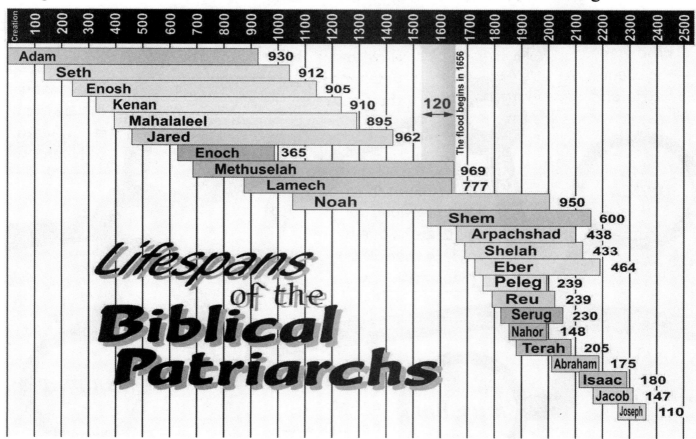

Start here

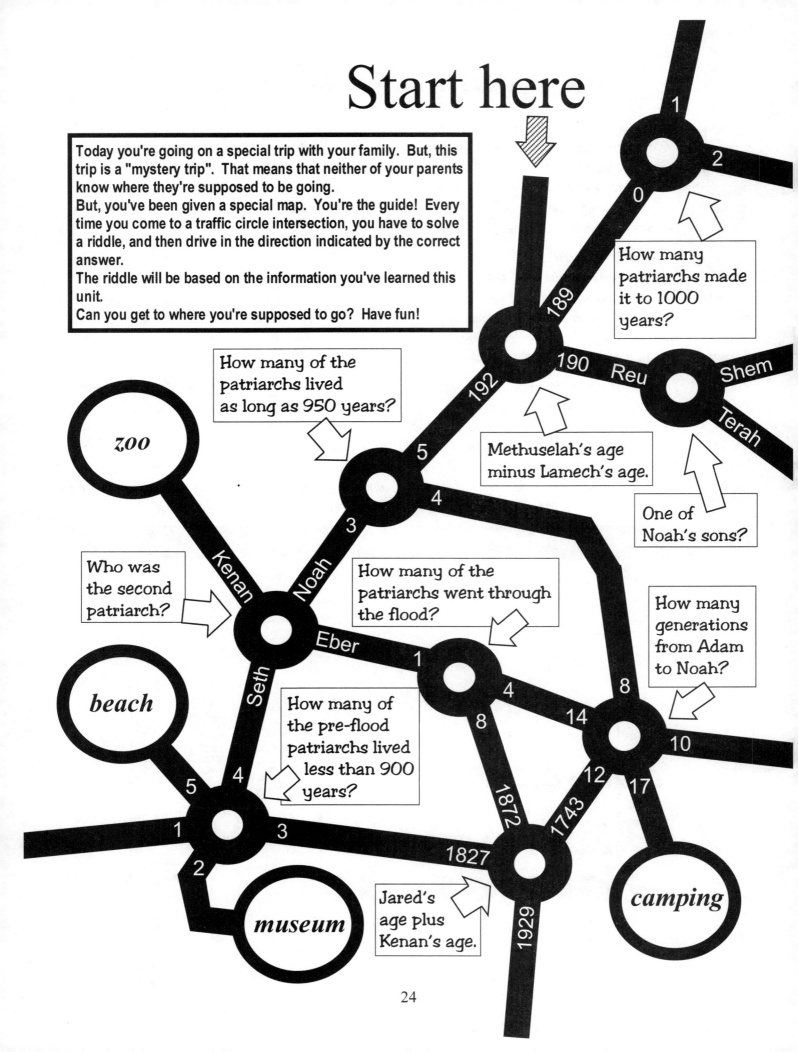

Today you're going on a special trip with your family. But, this trip is a "mystery trip". That means that neither of your parents know where they're supposed to be going.

But, you've been given a special map. You're the guide! Every time you come to a traffic circle intersection, you have to solve a riddle, and then drive in the direction indicated by the correct answer.

The riddle will be based on the information you've learned this unit.

Can you get to where you're supposed to go? Have fun!

How many patriarchs made it to 1000 years?

How many of the patriarchs lived as long as 950 years?

Methuselah's age minus Lamech's age.

One of Noah's sons?

Who was the second patriarch?

How many of the patriarchs went through the flood?

How many generations from Adam to Noah?

How many of the pre-flood patriarchs lived less than 900 years?

Jared's age plus Kenan's age.

zoo

beach

museum

camping

1 2 0
189 190 Reu Shem
192 Terah
5 4
3
Kenan Noah
Seth Eber
1 4 8
8 14
12 17
1872 1743 10
1827 1929
5 4
1 3
2

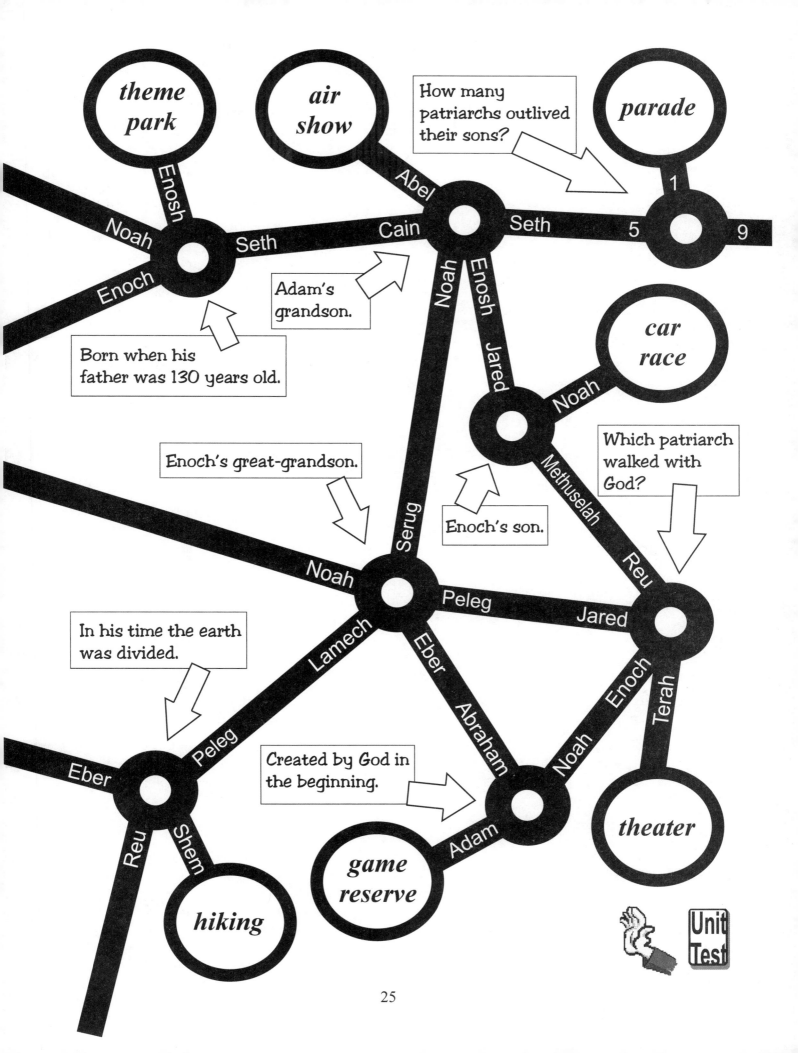

25

UNIT 3

THE FLOOD

Genesis 6 - 9

GOD'S PLAN: DESTRUCTION!

*W*e are now going to study a very important part of the CREATION MODEL – the great flood of Noah's time. This part <u>must</u> be included in any study of the origins of things on Earth because it played a major role in forming the earth that we have today. But, there are many people, of course, who say that the great flood is only a legend. They say it never happened and is just a fantasy. Other people say that there was a flood, but it only covered the Greater Mesopotamia area. In other words, they say it was only a much smaller, local flood.

Well, we're going to see that it was, in fact, GLOBAL. What does "global" mean? That means it covered the whole earth – the whole globe. Not only does the Bible teach this, but there is also amazing evidence around the world that this is so.

Let's first find out why there was a flood. It wasn't just an accident. It was purposely sent by God onto the earth to destroy it! Then we'll see how preparations were made.

✱ Read Chapter 6 of Genesis, then answer the following questions:

1. Verse 6 tells us that God is grieved. Why? (vs. 5, 11 & 12)_____

    _____

2. What does God decide to do? (vs. 7) _____

    _____

3. What was God going to destroy *in addition* to people? (vs. 13) _____

4. To whom does He tell this? (vss. 8 & 13) _____

5. Why did God choose this man? (vs. 9) _____

6. What did God tell him to do? (vs. 14) _____

7. What was he to coat the ark with, inside and out? (vs. 14) _____

8. How big was the ark to be? (vs. 15) Length:_____Width:_____Height:_____

9. How was Noah to collect the animals? (vs. 20) _____

10. How were the people and animals to get their food? (vs. 21) _____

Think about this: If the great flood of Noah's day was only a localized flood, there would have been no need for the ark. People and animals could simply walk away from the rising water.

THE ARK

*L*et's look a little closer at the ark that Noah built. This was an amazing vessel that carried eight people and a whole zoo through a terrible disaster for over a year. There are, of course, many people who say that the ark is just another "Bible fairy tale". These people come up with all sorts of reasons why they believe that the ark couldn't have done what the Bible says it did. Sometimes, even Christians begin to doubt the Bible's account when they hear these criticisms. So, it would be wise to look at the main arguments that people have against the ark, and answer them. Since you've already read the passage where God instructs Noah on how to build it, we won't read it again now – we'll just look at the arguments.

Argument # 1: *The ark wasn't big enough to carry all the animals.*

- **Answer**: Yes, it certainly *was* big enough. Do you remember the dimensions of the ark? It was 450 feet long, 75 feet wide, and 45 feet high. If you remember verse 16 from chapter 6, it says that there were 3 floors, or decks. Now, let's do some math. Each floor would have had 33,750 square feet of room. The ceilings on every floor were 15 feet high. That means there was a total of *at least* 1,500,000 cubic feet of room on the ark! What does that mean? Well, let's picture it in a different way. The picture you see on the right is of an average sized train boxcar. You've probably seen many of these when you've been stopped by a freight train. You know how big they are! Well, the ark was so big, that it could have held over **_500_** of these boxcars! That's a lot of space! Each one of these boxcars can hold

over 200 sheep-sized animals. Experts have figured out that most of the animal kinds could have fit on just two decks of the ark. The rest of the space would have been used by Noah and his family, and for food storage. The ark was a huge vessel, even compared to modern ships!

Here's something else to remember about the animals that Noah took with him on the ark. There are many people who think that the Bible teaches that Noah took two of every **SPECIES** of animal with him. He did not. The Bible says that he took two of every **KIND** of animal (and he was told to take seven of some kinds). What is the difference between a **SPECIES** and a **KIND**?

Well, to make this clear, let's look at dogs. If you saw a dog, you could say, "What **KIND** of animal is that?" The answer would be "a dog". That's what **KIND** of animal it is. But the dog might be a German Shepherd. That is its **SPECIES**. All species of dogs come from a kind. So, Noah possibly had one or several kinds of dogs on the ark, not all the many varieties (or species) we have today. All of the many varieties (species) of animals we have today came from the original created kinds. So, this greatly reduces the numbers of creatures that needed to be aboard.

One final note on the animals that were on the ark: Look at verse 17. It hints at something that is made clearer in the next chapter. It tells us that only creatures that have the breath of life in their nostrils were taken aboard the ark. Verse 20 also indicates that the creatures taken were birds, animals, and creatures that crawl on the ground. No mention of insects or fish. These could have survived outside the ark, even though many did die in the flood, of course (that's why we find fossils of them today).

Argument # 2: *Noah couldn't have fit the huge animals, like elephants, onto the ark.*

- **Answer**: Yes, he could have. Again, scientists have studied this question and have come up with an interesting conclusion. The *average* size of the creatures on the ark would have been about the size of a rat. Only about 11% of all the animals on the ark (that's 11 animals out of 100) would have been much bigger than a sheep. Also, Noah could have taken some young animals. Elephants, for example, are very large, but a young elephant would take up far less room.

Argument # 3: *The ark would not have been a very steady boat.*

- **Answer**: Yes, it would have been very steady. Tests done on models of the ark have proved that it would have been not only very steady, but also almost impossible to capsize.

Argument # 4: *Noah was not a shipbuilder, so he couldn't have built the ark.*

- **Answer**: Yes, he could have. Here's one reason why: Noah had 120 years to build it (see Genesis 6:3), and since he probably had help, this task certainly could be accomplished. There's another reason. But first, look at these two pictures below. Which one do you think looks more like the ark?

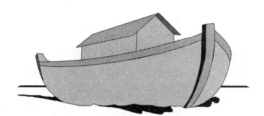 

If you guessed the one on the right, you're correct. The one on the left looks like a boat because that's what we're used to seeing today, but that's not the shape that Noah built. The word for "ark" in the Hebrew language (the language in which the Old Testament is written) does not mean "ship" or "boat". It means "box" or "coffin". All he was building was a large box. It wasn't going anywhere either. It was just designed to float, so it didn't need a special "pointed" front. It didn't leak because of the pitch that was used to coat it, inside and out (see verse 14).

Fill in the missing words:

1. Noah took two of every _____ of animal with him on the ark.

2. The ark was so big that it could have held _____(number) railroad boxcars.

3. How many floors, or decks did the ark have? _____

4. The only creatures taken on board were those that had the _____ in their nostrils.

5. Noah had _____ years to build the ark.

Circle the correct answer:

6. Noah took fish with him on the ark.   TRUE   FALSE

7. A "species" is the same as a "kind".   TRUE   FALSE

8. The ark looked more like a box than a ship.   TRUE   FALSE

9. The ark was coated with pitch to seal it.   TRUE   FALSE

THE FLOOD!

*B*esides sin, which caused God to curse the creation, the flood was the greatest event that gave us our earth as it appears today. We've seen that man was terribly wicked, and that God had to punish mankind. The flood was to be a terrible judgment on man. Chapter six of Genesis leads us up to this event. God has purposed to destroy living creatures and the earth. The ark is made, and the animals have come to Noah. As chapter six closes, we see that Noah has obeyed God. Now, the most terrible destruction ever to hit the earth is about to take place.

✱ *Read Chapter 7 of Genesis, then answer the following questions:*

1. How did Noah know exactly on which day the flood would start? (7:4) _____

_____

2. How old was Noah when the flood began? (7:6) _____

3. How many people were on the ark? (7:7 & 13) _____

4. On which day did the "fountains of the great deep" burst forth? (7:11)_____

_____

5. (*In order to answer this next question accurately, read II Peter 3:5–6, then go back to Genesis 7*)

   Where did the water for the flood come from? (7:11)_____

_____

6. How long did the rain fall? (7:12)_____

7. ***THINK!*** How do we know that many fish and insects *didn't* die in the flood? (7:22)

_____

8. ***THINK!*** How do we know that the entire earth was covered, and not just part of it? (7:19 - 20)

_____

9. How long did the waters flood (prevail, destroy, ravage) the earth? (7:24) _____

THE FLOOD RECEDES

*W*e can only imagine what all went on during the terrible events described in Genesis chapter seven. All over the world, horrible catastrophes were going on that nobody who survived in the ark was able to see. The earth was being ripped apart. Huge amounts of water were squirting out of the ground at tremendous speeds, and reaching at least 20 miles up into the sky. This water came down in the form of terrible, violent, dirty rains. High winds whipped up dust and debris. Mountains of water were not only falling from the sky, but also washing over the earth, killing everything in its path and burying things in sediment. As the earth ground and cracked, volcanic activity came into being, spewing dust, ash and lava into the already-choked air. Desperate people and animals tried to get away as best they could, but their escape was only very temporary. People who were about to die must have witnessed the most terrible sights imaginable. If you can picture in your mind the horrors that were going on, you would have a great sense of awe for the mighty God who judged the world by sending this disaster. God is truly a God of love, but He is also a God of righteousness and judgment.

Well, the flood did end, of course. God stopped the fountains of the deep, and things began to settle down. Let's read the next part of this story....

✱ *Read Chapter 8 of Genesis, then answer the following questions:*
Circle either "TRUE" or "FALSE".
<u>**(You'll have to work for these!**</u> *Hint: refer to chapter 7:11 for help on some of them.)*

1.	The rain fell for one hundred and fifty days.	TRUE	FALSE
2.	The water began to go down as soon as the rain stopped.	TRUE	FALSE
3.	There were five months from the time the flood started to the time the ark settled on Ararat.	TRUE	FALSE
4.	The valleys became visible 2 months after the ark settled.	TRUE	FALSE
5.	After the mountaintops became visible, Noah waited 40 more days before sending out the first bird.	TRUE	FALSE
6.	The first bird sent out was a raven.	TRUE	FALSE
7.	The other bird Noah sent out was a dove.	TRUE	FALSE
8.	One time, the dove brought back a fresh fig leaf.	TRUE	FALSE
9.	Altogether, Noah was on the ark 375 days.	TRUE	FALSE
10.	Everything on the ark had survived.	TRUE	FALSE

A NEW BEGINNING

*T*he judgment was over. The horrors of the flood were past. Noah, his family, and all the creatures on the ark came out and started life anew. The world looked very different now. Gone

were the huge, lush forests that covered much of the earth before the flood. Noah was looking at a barren, mountainous landscape, but one with new plant growth sprouting up everywhere.

In the next chapter, Noah and his family begin life in a strange place. He doesn't know where he is. Nothing looks familiar. Noah couldn't possibly know this, but the whole world was different now. In the New Testament, the apostle Peter refers to the world that perished in the flood as the "world that then was" or the "world that is gone". We'll see in the next lesson a bit more on this. Right now, let's look at the new beginning they were all faced with.

✳ Read Chapter 9 of Genesis, then answer the following questions:

1. What does God tell Noah and his family to do? (vs. 1) _____

2. Did animals fear man before the flood? (vs. 2) _____

3. What is mankind given permission to eat now? (vs. 3) _____

4. What must man *not* eat? (vs. 4) _____

5. Why is mankind so special? (vs. 6) _____

6. Because of this, what does God say must happen to a person who "sheds the blood of man"? (vs. 6)

   _____

7. What does God promise to people and animals in the new "covenant" he establishes? (vs. 8 – 11)

   _____

8. What did God give them as a sign of this promise? (vss. 12 – 17) _____

It is interesting to note that the very first response that Adam and Eve had to their sin in Eden was the realization that they were naked. They suddenly were very conscious of this, and they were ashamed. That's why they quickly made coverings for themselves and then hid from God. We can see in Genesis chapter 9:21 - 25 that this same shame was still in effect; that's why Noah cursed Ham's descendants – and it's more than 1,657 years since creation at this point!

Something to think about: In our society, shame over nakedness doesn't seem to bother people. What do you think that indicates about our society today? It seems that sin has so blinded people that they don't even sense their lost condition; they seem completely indifferent to it.

THE PHASES OF THE EARTH

It appears, from Scripture, that the earth has undergone many changes in the past. That is, it has looked very different at different points in history. We've attempted here to give you just an idea of what it might have looked like at these times.

There are two events in history that have caused these changes. The first is, of course, creation. When God spoke, things happened!! Things appeared! The earth was created.

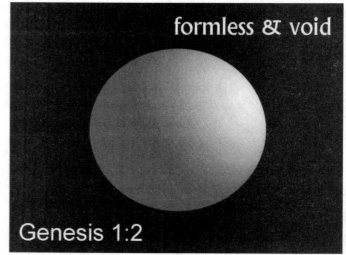

formless & void

Genesis 1:2

However, the event which caused the major changes on the earth was the flood. Some things changed rather quickly, while other things took some time.

Let's look at these events. The first one, which we call "formless and void", is found in the second verse of Genesis chapter one. When God first created the earth, there were no mountains, rivers, continents — or anything to give it a recognizable shape. It was "without form". The word "void" means "empty". God hadn't put anything there yet. At this point, the earth was covered by deep water. Everything was dark. Apparently, all the elements were there, but not yet organized or energized by God.

Then God spoke, and things began to happen — to be orderly. After creating light and energy, God did something on the second day which we still don't really understand. The Bible says that God "divided" water from water by putting a firmament (an expanse) between the waters. Some

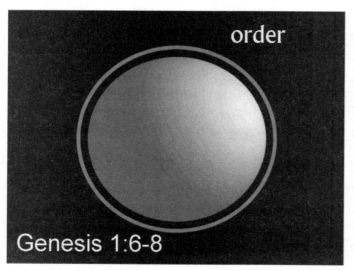

order

Genesis 1:6-8

scientists believe that this means that God made a "canopy" of water vapor or ice around the earth very high up in the sky, and that this canopy helped to shield the earth from harmful rays of the sun and perhaps make the earth a comfortable temperature all over. This may be partly correct.

However, some of them believe that when this canopy broke up at the time of the flood, it caused much of the rain and flooding on Earth. This is incorrect. The Bible makes it clear in Genesis 7, but especially in II Peter 3: 5-6, that the flood waters came from BELOW the earth

as the fountains of the great deep burst out. The water that shot way up into the sky came back down as violent rain. If there was some form of canopy, it did not cause the flood or even add much, if any, water to it, and it probably disappeared at the time of the flood.

Again God spoke, and the earth changed. He sent the water to one place so that dry ground would appear. The dry ground He called "land" and the water He called "seas". But, this isn't all He did on the third day of creation. He also caused the land to produce vegetation: seed-bearing plants and trees.

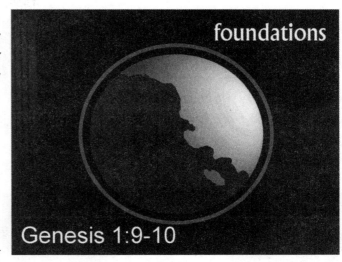

foundations

Genesis 1:9-10

We call this phase the "foundation" phase. Why? Vegetation is absolutely vital to the existence of other living creatures. For one thing, vegetation was to be the food that all animals ate. Even man was given "every herb bearing seed...and every tree, in which is the fruit of a tree yielding seed" to eat. For another thing, vegetation produces oxygen — very vital to our survival! Trees and plants are also designed to help keep the air clean .

After laying this foundation, God continued with His creation until all of it was finished to perfection — in six days. Well, as you know, man sinned and brought a curse from God. But the

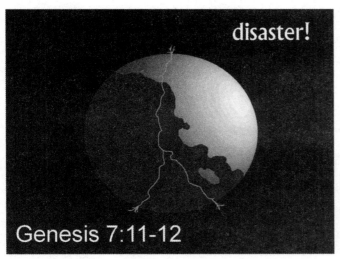

disaster!

Genesis 7:11-12

world itself looked the same for about 1,656 years, until God had finally had enough and decided to punish man — through a global flood! This event changed the earth again.

Now, we don't exactly know how God brought this about. Some people have suggested that He sent a giant asteroid that hit the earth and caused the start of the crack-up of the earth's crust. Perhaps this is what happened. Others have suggested that the core of the earth began to swell, and this caused the crust of the earth to crack up and let the deep waters out. We really don't know. These are just ideas. Anyway, the crack would have circled all over the earth's crust very quickly (in just hours!) at the weakest points. Then the fountains of the deep (which were HUGE reservoirs of interconnected water chambers containing perhaps as much as half of the water that is in our oceans today) erupted from these cracks because of the weight of the crust pushing down on the deep waters. We do know that, whatever started it, the waters pouring out of the cracks caused massive amounts of erosion against the walls of the earth's crust. All of this eroded material produced the sediments all over the world (we'll read about that in the next lesson). The earth was quickly becoming a disaster zone. Everything was being ripped up, killed, buried — destroyed!

This part of the disaster phase lasted for 40 days. The water was pouring out of the cracks high up into the atmosphere and returning as rain. During that time, the rain was terrible! In Hebrew, it is called "geshem" rain. This is extremely violent, like you would find in a tornado or hurricane. Some of the water, because of the height to which it was blown, came back down in the form of massive ice dumps which trapped and quickly froze many animals, including the mammoths.

Have you ever seen a caterpillar turning into a butterfly or moth? Actually, nobody has! It takes place in secret. The transformation is amazing. The creature starts off looking like a worm, then goes through a mysterious change inside a cocoon or chrysalis. It comes out looking nothing at all like it used to. It's a new creature.

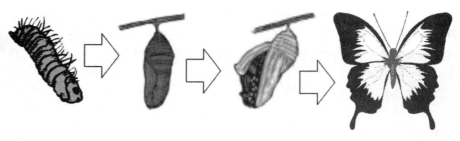

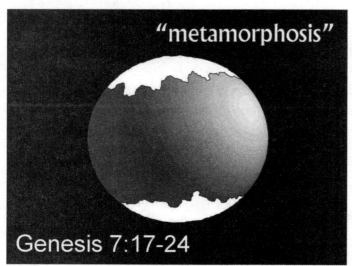

"metamorphosis"

Genesis 7:17-24

In a similar way, the earth underwent a change during the flood. The Bible says that the entire earth was covered by water. We know that the processes that produced the flood ripped the earth apart. The land masses shifted around on top of what was left of the fountains of the deep. Volcanic activity erupted all over as whole continents ground to a halt. Mountains rose up as the continents buckled. Much, if not most, of this metamorphosis took place during the forty days of rain.

Now, the next step of the earth's transformation began. New, deep ocean trenches had been formed where the continents had slid apart. The floodwaters now began to drain into these. This began as soon as the rain stopped (Genesis 8:2-3). By the end of the 150 days of flooding, the water had gone down enough that the ark was able to settle in Ararat. Of course, at this point, only five months had passed since the flood began. Noah, his family, and all the animals would have to sit in the ark on the mountain for about another seven months! During this time, the water steadily drained from the earth into the oceans. Dry land reappeared, but it still didn't look like the earth we have today. Huge polar caps had formed and the "ice age" began. New weather patterns had come into existence. At this point, as Noah was allowed to come off of the ark, the continents were all larger than they appear today. Also, they were all connected because the oceans were lower then. This is important because of what we will study in the last lesson in this chapter, "The Nations".

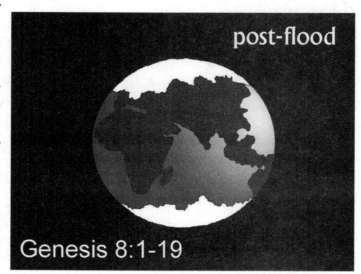

post-flood

Genesis 8:1-19

We have called this phase the "post-flood" phase. "Post" means "after", so right after the flood, and perhaps for the next several hundred years or more, the earth continued to slowly change again, this time taking us up to the way the earth looks today.

The final phase of the earth took place over a long period of time. Forces resulting from the flood were still at work, but at a much slower pace. We have called this phase, "home". The current look

Genesis 10:25

of the earth is familiar to us and changes very little now. What brought about this final change?

The oceans were much lower right after the flood than they are today. This caused most of the land masses to still be connected. For example, England was still connected to Europe; Japan and Australia were still connected to Asia; Alaska was still connected to Siberia, etc. (see "post flood").

But, something was causing the oceans to rise steadily. Some scientists think this was due to several things at one time. First, the continents were "settling". They had been made much thicker during the flood due to all the sediments on top of them (the mountains were also higher at that time than they are now). As they settled into the layer of the earth immediately beneath them, they forced the ocean floors upward. This made the surface of the ocean rise, too.

Another possible cause that some scientists believe added to this rise was melting icecaps. The icecaps started forming during the flood and became much larger after the flood (and much larger than they are today). This is what produced the one "ice age" our earth has experienced. As these huge caps melted, they added water to the already-rising oceans. Eventually, as the water rose up the sides of the continents, called the CONTINENTAL SLOPE *(Figure 1), it began to move inland up the* CONTINENTAL SHELF. *The higher the oceans rose, the more they began to flood the low-lying parts of the dry land (Figure 2). This is how our modern-day continents formed.*

Is there any evidence of this from the Bible? Possibly. In Genesis 10:25, a man is born who is given the name "Peleg". This name means "divided" and some people who have studied this name think that it means, "divided by water". If so, then perhaps when Peleg was born, 101 years after the flood, this process of the oceans rising had already begun, and could be observed. The continents were being born as they were separated by slowly rising oceans. Others think that Peleg was given this name because he might have been born at the time people were scattering after Babel.

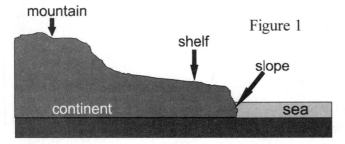

mountain

Figure 1

shelf

slope

continent   sea

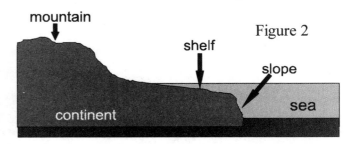

mountain

Figure 2

shelf

slope

continent   sea

NOTE -- Teacher: Some of the above (concerning the flood) was inspired by the *Hydroplate Theory*, proposed by Dr. Walter Brown in his book, *In The Beginning*. Biblically accurate and scientifically plausible, this theory is a very possible scenario that explains the flood and its aftermath. However, there are other theories, too. True creation scientists agree about all of the major aspects of the flood (e.g. it was global, a judgment on sin, produced the layered strata and the current continents, etc.). Sometimes they differ with each other somewhat on exactly *how* it might have happened because the Bible is silent on the issue. In these cases, it's good to remember that researchers have some latitude in their opinions and conclusions.

FLOOD EVIDENCE TODAY

*A*s mentioned before, there are many people who doubt that there was a worldwide flood. They say that it's just a legend. Well, let's imagine, for a few minutes, that you had never read about the flood in the Bible, and nobody had ever told you about it. Now, let's look at just a few strange things about our earth, and see what could possibly explain how they got there.

First, let's consider our neighbor out in space, Mars. Many scientists have become very excited about the possibility that there might be, or might have been, life on Mars. This is wrong, of course, but the reason they think this is because some areas on the surface of Mars look as if moving water existed there at some time in the past. And, there might have been! There isn't any now. But, they look at these patterns (that look like rivers once flowed there) and say, "Wow! Mars must have been covered by water at one time!" It's interesting that they would say that about a planet that has NO LIQUID WATER on it today. But then, what about our earth?   It is still a "water planet" because it is still <u>74% covered by water</u>, but these scientists say that it was never completely covered. Why?

Next, let's look at fossils. Earth has many high mountain ranges, and many fossils can be found on and in them. What if we would find MARINE fossils on these mountains? (MARINE creatures live in water.) What if we would find <u>billions</u> of marine fossils on <u>all</u> the mountain ranges? Well, guess what? — WE DO!   Wouldn't it be reasonable to assume then that, at some point in the past, these areas were under water? If not, then how would you explain how they came to be there, and in such huge numbers?

Then there's the question of STRATA. You might not have heard of that word before, but most of us have seen them. Have you ever traveled in a mountainous region before? Perhaps you've been through areas where the mountain had to be cut away to make room for the road you're on. Sometimes you can see the strata clearly on the mountain. It looks like different colored lines of rock. Sometimes the lines are parallel to the

ground; other times they go up at an angle; sometimes they bend like an "S". Here's a picture of clear strata on a mountainside.

Well, what are they, and how did they get there? Strata are rock that have been laid down in layers. These layers are known as SEDIMENTARY LAYERS. Sediments are laid down by water. So, the strata that we see on mountains were put there during a large water event, like a flood. The reason that some of them go up at angles is because they were pushed into that position when mountains formed. They were pushed up during the flood (more of this in the next lesson).

Now, here are some interesting things to observe about these strata. First, there is no EROSION between the layers, or very little. Erosion is caused by wind and water taking away the soil. If these strata layers were put there over billions of years, as the evolutionists believe, then we would see massive amounts of erosion BETWEEN the layers all over the world. Furthermore, we should see evidence of TOPSOIL between the layers. This would have been absolutely necessary to grow plants throughout these long time periods. But, we see neither erosion nor topsoil between the layers! Why? The only logical answer is that the layers were placed there either at the same time, or very rapidly.

Another interesting point to consider is POLYSTRATE FOSSILS. This is a big word made up of two words. "Poly" means "more than one", and "strate" means "strata". Therefore, this particular kind of fossil crosses many strata. Look at the fossil tree at the right. It's going through many sedimentary layers. It's impossible for the tree to grow in one spot, then die, and then stand there for thousands or millions of years while layers slowly built all around it. It would have rotted away long before it would have been covered.

No, the tree was buried rapidly by a water event that carried lots of sediment in it. Does this show that the world was under water at one point? Of course not, but since there are many fossils of this kind around the world, it at least shows that there was rapid burial of these trees and other polystrate fossils.

One other point we want to consider is the worldwide story of a great, global, water event. All over the world there are various cultures of people, many of whom have a very limited knowledge, if any, of the world outside just their own community. Some of these people are tribal and live deep in the jungles. Others are more modern. But, there are over 270 separate people groups around the world that include as part of their culture, a story from the distant past of a global flood. All of these cultures say that a very few people survived this event – in some sort of boat or island.

If you had <u>never</u> heard the story of Noah, what would you think about the evidence presented above? What would YOU think happened on the earth at some point in the past? Write it down.

_____

_____

_____

✱ _Now, consider this interesting point:_ Based only on the evidence we've just seen, most scientists would believe that the earth somehow had been totally covered by water at some time in the past. But, many of them deny it because the account of such an event is found in the Bible!

FOSSILS

*W*e've mentioned fossils several times in the last lessons, so let's take a bit of a closer look at fossils, what they are, where they come from, and what formed them. First, look at the fossils here on this page. They're from different ORGANISMS that were alive at some time in the past. An organism is a plant or animal that has various parts that all work together to help it survive. There are fossils of many different animals and plants.

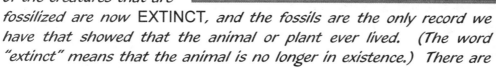

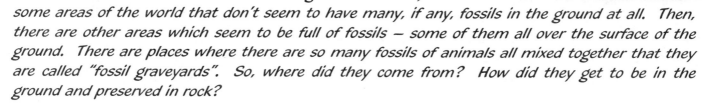

A fossil is the hardened remains or imprint of plant or animal life preserved in rock. Some of the creatures that are fossilized are now EXTINCT, and the fossils are the only record we have that showed that the animal or plant ever lived. (The word "extinct" means that the animal is no longer in existence.) There are some areas of the world that don't seem to have many, if any, fossils in the ground at all. Then, there are other areas which seem to be full of fossils — some of them all over the surface of the ground. There are places where there are so many fossils of animals all mixed together that they are called "fossil graveyards". So, where did they come from? How did they get to be in the ground and preserved in rock?

First of all, it is important to understand that fossils rarely form today. When a creature dies, it DECOMPOSES quickly. That means that the animal rots, or decays; its soft parts quickly disappear, and what's left gets eaten up by tiny organisms long before they are buried in enough sediments to preserve their shapes. The only way that a plant or animal can be fossilized is by being buried very rapidly. And, in some cases, it's even very clear to see that this happened. Take the case of this creature below, for example. It's an ichthyosaur. Like many fossils, you can clearly

see most of her. She was buried very rapidly right at the moment she was giving birth to a baby, which you can clearly see at the back.

The Geological Column...

Evolutionists point to all the sedimentary layers (the strata) and say that they were deposited, or placed where they are, over many millions of years. Then, they divide up these sediments into "ages", and then give them names. They say that the sediments trapped the animals alive at the time the sediment was placed there, and many of these animals became fossils. Then, you can trace evolution through millions of years of time by following their "fossil record". They even have a chart that illustrates their belief. They call it "The Geological Column". You can see it here to the right.

On the far left side of the chart are the names of each of the "ages". Then you can see a drawing of the layered strata (the sedimentary layers of rock). To the right of that you can see drawings of animals that SUPPOSEDLY have been found in that particular layer. So, if you want to know when evolutionists say that fish evolved, you find a drawing of a fish, or look at the description at the far right of the column, then look to the left, and you can see the "age" in which it lived (or first appeared), and how long ago it was.

If you want to find out when they say that dinosaurs roamed the earth, you follow the same steps. However, is the information accurate? NO!

This chart is actually very old, but it is still used today. Evolutionists drew it long ago, and it shows what they HOPED, or THOUGHT, they would find if they were able to dig into the sediments. Well, guess what?! They never found it. In fact, in many places around the world, the "ages" are in the wrong positions. That means that fossils that supposedly show more "modern", or highly evolved creatures, are often found UNDER the fossils of animals from which they supposedly evolved!! In fact, many people who believe in evolution are frustrated because the fossil record does NOT show what they thought it should if their theory of evolution is correct.

So, what happened? Where do fossils come from? For the most part, they came from the flood, which trapped billions and billions of animals and plants and preserved their images in rock for us to see today. The fossil record is a reminder to us that there was indeed a judgment — a worldwide flood, and that God means business when He says that He hates sin.

Speaking of judgment on sin, it is important for us to read a passage of Scripture that tells us more of this....because there is another judgment on the way!

✳ *Read II Peter 3:3-7, then answer the following questions:*

1. What are some people deliberately forgetting (or willfully ignorant of)? _____

_____

2. What was the earth formed of, or founded upon? _____

3. How were the heavens and earth formed? _____

4. By what was the earth destroyed? _____

5. What is going to happen to the present heavens and earth? _____

_____

6. Why is this going to happen? _____

7. Who will cause this to happen? And, how? _____

These verses indicate that the flood completely buried the "world of that time" (the earth that "then was" KJV). We know now that this includes being buried in sediments. So, the creation view of the "geological column" is that it didn't take hundreds of millions of years to form — it took just several months! The "world of that time" (that means, before the flood) is at the bottom of the chart. The world upon which Adam walked is at the bottom. The rest of the chart simply represents the sediment layers laid down by the flood. This is why it's impossible to know where Eden was. It's buried....somewhere! The Mesopotamia region is generally called the "Cradle of Civilization" (that's why some people think Eden was there), but that's because civilization began there again AFTER THE FLOOD. This region is near where the ark came to rest.

Verse 7 of this passage is what we want to focus on now. The Bible makes it clear that there is another horrible judgment coming. God promised that He would never again destroy the earth with a flood, but the next judgment will be by fire! Very few people escaped the first judgment. People of Noah's time mocked and laughed at the warnings given to them. They paid for this terribly!

What about you? Are you ready for the next judgment?

God is gracious. He doesn't want people to perish. He wants people to live with Him forever in a perfect place with no problems — heaven! But, we can only get there through faith in His son, Jesus, who created everything, and then bought it back through paying the debt we owed, but couldn't pay, by the shedding of His own blood.

THE NATIONS

*W*e're coming to the end of our studies in the book of Genesis. So far, we've been looking at the "launching pad" of our earth and its inhabitants – the first eleven chapters. We've seen history from day #1 up to the birth of Abram. This covers 2008 years!

We will look at the nations of the world now, and how they came to be. We'll see how Noah's sons produced many children and grandchildren, and that from these people the nations spread out over the earth after the flood. But, that's not quite the end of the story yet. There are still a few more interesting events. Let's read about them.

✳ Read Genesis 10, and 11: 1 - 9, and then answer the following questions:

1. Who was the great warrior & hunter who founded the cities of Babylon and Nineveh? _____

2. How many languages were there up to this time? _____

3. What was the name of the plain into which some people moved? _____

4. What did they decide to build there? _____

5. What building materials did they use? _____

6. Why did they want to build this? _____

_____

7. What two things did God do to stop them? _____

_____

Finish the six questions first, then continue here.....

*I*t's very interesting to note why God confused their language. He did it because He knew that man could accomplish huge amounts of tasks if they could understand each other and operate as a team! God said that nothing would be impossible for them. And, why not? We are made in the very image of God. That means that mankind is creative, inventive, and ingenious. We can accomplish great things and figure out solutions to problems. In this regard, we are much higher than the animal world. Animals operate from instinct (we'll learn more about this in a later lesson), but man has to learn everything. Man has very little instinct.

God confused the language and did one other thing, too. He scattered mankind throughout the world (up to this point, man was only living in the present-day, Middle-East region of the world). How did He move people over the face of the whole earth? The Bible doesn't say. He could perhaps have done it by a miracle. It could be, though, that the flood again provides an answer.

Remember that the flood basically created new continents. Immediately after the floodwaters went down, the oceans were much lower. Remember, too, that this would have caused all the

present-day continents to be still joined together. What does that suggest to you as a possible way that God moved people over the whole earth? Look at the map to the right. There's something odd about it, right? Africa looks pretty much the same, but look at South America. Where's England? Where's Japan? Look at North America and Siberia.....they're connected!

You see, with the oceans lowered just 200 – 400 feet, all the continents are still connected, and it would look pretty much like this. This would have given a perfect "land bridge" for people to cross as God spread them over all the earth from Shinar (or, Babylonia, where the white dot is). Animals also migrated to various parts of the world this way.

Remember that God had confused the language. Now people couldn't understand each other. It seems likely that people who COULD understand each other probably stayed together as they moved. This would greatly reduce the ability of these small groups of people to pass down to their children certain features that the other groups might have. For example, someone in one group might have had the ability to grow very blonde hair, and the next group might have had someone with the ability to grow black hair. These, and many other abilities (such as how tall a person will grow, the color of their skin, the shape of their nose, the color of their hair, etc.) are controlled by a special code in each person called the GENETIC CODE. This is how the various "races" of people eventually appeared.

Now, look at this next map. The black parts are our current continents. The grey is the area of land that flooded as the oceans slowly rose. The edge of the grey is the edge of the "shelf" where each continent actually ends. As the oceans rose, the water covered these low-lying parts, giving us our present-day continents. This

is why some animals are unique to certain areas of the world – kangaroos in Australia, giraffes in Africa, etc. They, too, became isolated on whatever land they were as the waters slowly rose. (If certain animals, like kangaroos for example, lived elsewhere, they perhaps died off over time leaving the only survivors in Australia where they now thrive.) This, then, was the birth of the nations of the world stemming from Noah's sons.

The Creation Model

You have just studied, over these last 3 units, the basic ideas behind the CREATION MODEL. As stated before, the creation model is best understood as a series of events that happened over many years, not just during the "creation week". The creation model is a combination of all of the events, revealed to us in the Bible, that give us our world as we know it today. This includes the spiritual world and the PHYSICAL world (which is what we can see, smell, touch, taste and hear).

There are seven events that have occurred in history that are most important to understanding the creation model. All that we understand about the history of the earth and mankind revolve around these seven events. Likewise, the Christian world-view depends on these events being literal and true. To make this easy to remember, I have called this "The Seven Cs of the Creation Model".

1. CREATION – The creation week (Genesis 1 & 2)
2. CORRUPTION or CURSE – The fall of man (Genesis 3)
3. CATASTROPHE or CATACLYSM – The flood (Genesis 6-9)
4. CIVILIZATIONS or CULTURES – The nations (Genesis 4, 5 & 10)
5. CONFUSION – The events at Babel (Genesis 11)
6. COVENANT – The covenant with Abraham (Genesis 12)
7. CROSS – The cross (Matthew 27-28; Mark 15-16; Luke 23-24; John 19-20)

The "creation week" gives us our understanding of where everything came from right in the beginning, and the nature of all things as God originally created them.

The "fall of man" tells us why man is in the condition he is in today. It tells us why man is ALIENATED (separated) from God. It is the origin of all that is bad in the world today, including the fact that nature itself "groans" (Romans 8:22). This event brought about the necessity for mankind's need to be saved and REDEEMED (bought back) from the result of this original sin.

The "flood" brought into existence much of what we see on Earth today. Weather patterns (hail, tornadoes, hurricanes, etc.), the mountain ranges of the world, strata layers, the current continents, etc., are some examples of this. The flood changed the world physically from its original condition.

The "nations" & "events at Babel" are the origins of the different languages spoken all over the world. Also, the various racial groups can trace their origins back to this event since God spread mankind over the whole earth after confusing their language and separating them.

God's "covenant" with Abraham established the line of people that led to the nation of Israel. From these people came Jesus himself (see Luke 3). Much of the unrest in the world today, especially in the Middle-East countries, stems from the results of this covenant and the animosity between the sons of Isaac and Ishmael, both Abraham's sons.

The "cross" is the final important event in the history of the creation model. God, through His son Jesus, provided redemption for the lost sons of Adam (you & me!) and saves from the penalty of their sin those who trust in Him. Much of the history of the world revolves around those who have believed in this GOSPEL (good news) message, and carried it to others around the globe.

AN INTERESTING QUESTION --- *Many people have been curious to know why there are so few fossilized human bones found in the sedimentary layers. It's a good question, and there might be a relatively simple answer. First of all, it's true — there are very few, but there are indeed some. The probable reason that there are so few is that people are intelligent enough not only to see what was happening when the flood started, but also to get to higher ground. Only people would know the properties of water -- that it always finds the lowest point. People would have the knowledge that to survive, they'd need to get higher. So, probably most of them went up into high, pre-flood hills to escape rising water, and thus would escape the fossilization process. Some undoubtedly developed other means of temporarily escaping the rising water. Many, if not most, animals would have no idea what's going on, nor what to do. They'd simply drown. Any creatures that would have wound up as floating bodies (as was probably the case with most humans) would simply have rotted away, and whatever was left was eaten by microscopic creatures. There would be no remains!*

This is also probably why fossilized birds are rare, too. They have hollow bones for the most part, and so their bodies would have floated much easier. Most could have survived for a while anyway since they simply could stay in the air for long periods, or at least up in trees. Not so most animals.

The possible reasons why we don't see as many mammal fossils as dinosaur fossils are....
1) Mammals might have been much rarer. Dinosaurs might have multiplied very quickly, and so they might have been very dominant before the flood. Also, remember that large dinosaurs (whose fossils are actually fairly rare) had large bones, so their huge, fossilized bones would be much easier to find today.
2) It's also possible that certain mammals were more intelligent (to a degree) than dinosaurs and might have also been able to escape longer by finding higher ground.
3) Remember, too, that well over 90% of fossils (some say over 99%!) are marine creatures.

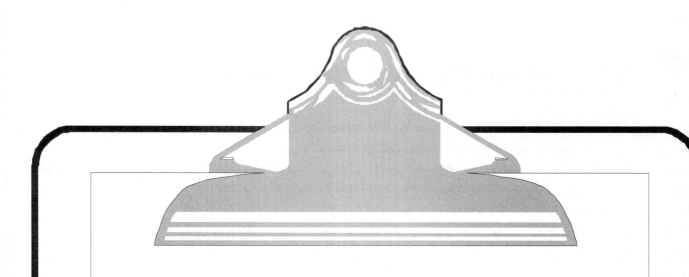

UNIT 4

SCIENCE VERSUS EVOLUTION

A LOOK AT "SCIENCE"

We're going to turn our attention now to the teachings of evolution. This will be just a brief study to help you understand the basic ideas behind the THEORY of evolution. A theory is a set of statements that attempt to explain something. Evolution is an attempt to explain the existence of everything apart from the Bible and apart from God creating it. It's a good idea to know what this theory is about because we live in a world full of people who believe in evolution (and what you believe about origins affects everything else in your life).

First of all, it's important to remember that people who believe in evolution say that it is based in science. They say that science establishes that evolution is true, so evolution is often taught as though it is a fact. So, let's look at the word SCIENCE and see what it means. Then, we'll apply that to evolution and see what science actually shows us.

Webster's dictionary says that science is: "knowledge, as distinguished from ignorance or misunderstanding". That simply means that if you've <u>never</u> heard of something, or don't know anything about it, you would be "ignorant" of it. But, if you <u>have heard</u> of something, or are aware of it, and arrive at wrong ideas about it, that's "misunderstanding".

The word "science" simply means "knowledge". If you say you have "knowledge" about something, and say that it's based in "science", you have to be able to provide solid evidence, or proof. Science is really the process of solving problems. The "scientific method" is the process by which scientists attempt to find answers to questions, or solutions to problems. There are three basic steps in the quest for scientific knowledge. 1) First, you have to identify the problem - you have to know what the problem is that you're trying to solve. 2) Then, you eventually come up with a workable idea, a theory, that you think will solve this problem. These steps can take a long time. 3) Finally, you have to test your idea to see if it works.

Let's imagine that you are a doctor who is looking for a cure for a disease. Using the "scientific method", you would obtain all the information you can about the disease (the problem), and then develop a cure (or, a theory about what will make the sick people get better). But, you don't know if it will work, so you will have to test it. How will you test it? You will have to find many people who have the disease and try your cure on them.

But, what if your theory doesn't work? You try it over and over again on many different patients, but nobody gets better. Would you say that you have found the cure? No, of course not. The scientific method has shown that your theory doesn't work, and you will have to start all over and try again.

This is how modern science works. You get "knowledge" through performing tests on your theory. A science theory must be "falsifiable" through the tests. These tests must be:

- **DEMONSTRABLE** – It must be able to be shown to others by clear evidence and examples.
- **REPEATABLE** – It must be able to be shown again and again.
- **OBSERVABLE** – It must be able to be seen, or witnessed.

If a theory does <u>not</u> meet these requirements, IT IS NOT TRUE SCIENCE, and it remains just a guess, a hope, a wishful thought – and it's then based on nothing but FAITH.

If you had a disease, would you take medicine for it that had been shown to NEVER work on your disease?

At this time, we're going to do a little experiment that will illustrate the points we've made about science and observation. You will need just a few items for this experiment. First, read the story below. It came from a "science" article in a newspaper and is changed a bit from the original to make it easier to understand.

Icebergs are floating mountains of ice that are drifting in the polar seas of the world. They can be very large and weigh millions of tons. Sometimes they drift into the shipping lanes of the North Atlantic Ocean and become dangerous obstacles. (The *Titanic* sank after striking one.)

Scientists are watching one such iceberg that measures 48 miles long and 22 miles wide. That's a HUGE piece of ice! They're concerned because it could affect the climate of the whole world. Why? Heat coming from the sun is reflecting off the iceberg and back into space. But, where rocks are exposed, it is absorbing the heat and causing the iceberg to melt and break up. This "melting and breaking up" of the iceberg is happening faster than the scientists expect. And, they say, if this condition continues, this huge mountain of floating ice could cause serious flooding all over the world .

✱ Collect these items:

- Glass cup (must be clear glass)
- At least 5 ice cubes
- <u>water-based</u> magic marker, felt pen, or highlighter

The main point of the story above is that if the iceberg melts too fast, it's going to cause serious flooding. So, let's see what actually happens when ice is placed in water.

- First, fill the glass about half full with water (the water represents the ocean). (Figure 1)
- Take your felt pen and draw a line where the level of the water is. (at arrow - Figure 1)
- Now, add the ice cubes (which represent the iceberg).
- Draw another line at the new water level. (at arrow – Figure 2)
- Now, answer these questions?
    1. When you added the ice cubes, which way did the water level go? Up or down?
    2. Is most of the ice ABOVE the new water level, or BELOW it?
    3. Let the ice melt. Did the water level go up, or down?

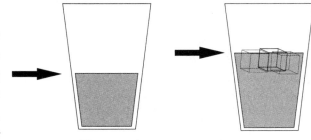

Figure 1   Figure 2

By doing this little experiment, you were testing a science theory, and by answering those three simple questions, you can easily see that the newspaper story was WRONG. Here's why: When the ice was added, the water rose to a new level. The ice floated on the surface of the water, but most of it was below the new water level. Pretend now that the water in the cup is the ocean, and the ice is the iceberg. If the iceberg is already in the ocean, THE WATER HAS ALREADY GONE UP! If the coastal cities of the world did not flood when the iceberg went into the ocean, they're certainly not going to flood when the ice melts! If anything, the water level is going to go BACK DOWN (what happened when your ice melted?). And, it certainly doesn't make any difference at all how fast the ice melts.

This is a good reminder to <u>not</u> believe everything you read.

THE PILLARS OF EVOLUTION

We've seen basically what science is. Now, let's look at the people who are called scientists. In a way, we're all scientists because we're curious about things, and we look for answers that work to solve problems or figure out ways of doing things. But, there are people who do this for a living. These people study problems, and many of them have discovered wonderful solutions to all kinds of problems. Building bridges involves science. Discovering cures for illnesses involves science. Sending rockets into space involves science. Almost everything we see around us involves science to some degree.

There are limits to science, of course. If something can't be measured, observed or demonstrated, no definite, scientific conclusions can be made. For example, did anyone see God create the world? Did anyone see how He did it? Can anyone observe His methods? No, of course not. Therefore, we cannot call creation "science", because we can't observe it happening. We have to accept it by faith. But, we don't accept it "blindly", that is, without evidence. There is much evidence that there is a God who created, but it still must be accepted by faith. Creation isn't a science theory; it's a biblical assertion.

But, Darwinian evolution, as a theory, has a major scientific problem -- It is not something that can be observed or demonstrated. It too must be accepted by faith. Why, then, are there scientists and teachers who say that evolution is a scientific fact? Another question to ask is: Why do so many people believe these scientists? Well, part of the reason is that many people think that scientists are always honest about what they discover. They think that scientists are always looking for the truth, and will share what they have learned, and admit it if they discover that their theory about the problem was wrong.

It would be nice if all scientists were that way. Most probably are, but when it comes to the explanation about where everything came from, there are many scientists who believe Darwinian evolution solidly and then claim that scientific observations and tests have proved it beyond doubt. This is absolutely false. Some do this because they really don't want to believe in God. They don't want to believe in creation - it sounds like a fairy tale to them. They don't want to believe that there was a flood. They don't want to follow God's laws. They, like many people, want to live life the way THEY want to live it. Since mankind are sinners, many like to stay in their sin and they don't want to change.

Many scientists believe it only because it's what they themselves were taught in school and in college, and they never really thought about it much. Many don't even know the major problems with evolution, nor much about creation. Still others accept evolution ONLY because they have to if they're going to keep their jobs! That's right! In some places, the scientists would be fired, or be placed in a much lower position, if they said they didn't believe in evolution.

THE SCIENTIST
*Always honest
*Always objective
*Never biased
*Infallible
(is this true?)

There are, of course, many scientists who do believe in the Bible and the creation. They see no conflict with the evidence for creation and good science. In fact, some of the greatest scientists who have ever lived were Christians who believed the Bible and the account of creation.

There are a lot of parts to the whole theory of evolution, so we've divided them up into basic areas. We're going to apply the rules of science to each of these major areas and see what we find out.

You'll notice that we have it drawn a bit like a temple. The roof is called EVOLUTION, and it is supported by three main pillars. The first one is called BIG BANG. The next is called LIFE FROM NON-LIFE. The last is called SIMPLE TO COMPLEX. These three pillars are placed on a foundation called TIME - *lots* of time! Each of these pillars will be briefly explained in the next few lessons. First, though, we need to look at the story of evolution in the simplest way, and then look at each of the parts.

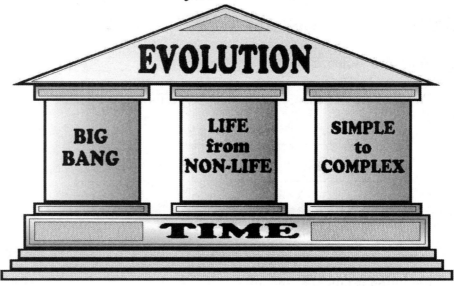

Billions of years ago, there was nothing in the universe. There were no stars, no moons, no planets, no oceans, no trees, no animals – nothing!....*except*.....one little ball or speck of something. Some scientists say that it was as small as the head of a pin; others say it was bigger. Anyway, suddenly, this ball exploded sixteen billion years ago. Over the next billions of years, the dust and gas from this little ball exploding began to form stars, and then galaxies. (This is the BIG BANG part.)

One star began to throw off pieces of itself. The pieces began to circle the star and turn hard as they cooled off. One of those pieces was our earth. Somehow, water came onto Earth and our oceans formed. In the oceans were many, many chemicals. About 4½ billion years ago, millions of these chemicals somehow, by chance, locked themselves together in a perfect way. By chance they formed a "skin" around themselves for protection and together became the first cell -- the first living thing, and somehow (again by chance) found something to eat. (This is the LIFE FROM NON-LIFE part.)

Somehow, this little single-celled creature was able to REPRODUCE itself. That means that it was able to make more of itself. This kept happening over and over. Somehow, in some of the new cells, other amazing changes started taking place that made the cell become more COMPLEX. That means that more parts were added that made the cell's whole system more complicated, better, and more functional. Eventually, some cells changed, getting better and better, over billions of years, to eventually become trees and plants. Other cells changed, getting better and better, over billions of years, to eventually become bugs and insects. Still other cells changed, getting better and better, over billions of years, to eventually become animals and finally....people! (This is the SIMPLE-TO-COMPLEX part.)

Evolutionists have drawn charts that they say give us a picture of this. Under charts like this one at left, it will often say something like this: "This chart shows how man evolved from a single-celled organism." Does it? No it doesn't. We'll see why later.

✱ *Let's do a quick review before we get into the details of each of the pillars of evolution.*

Fill in the missing words:

1. The word "science" means _____.

2. To try to prove a theory, tests must be performed which are...

    a. _____

    b. _____

    c. _____

3. If a theory does not, or cannot, pass these tests, it must be accepted by _____.

4. Evolution is taught as though it is a _____, but it is only an unproven _____.

5. The three major "pillars" (main events or turning points) of evolution are...

    a. _____

    b. _____

    c. _____

6. **The necessary foundation for all of the pillars of evolution to be true is lots of _____.**

THE BIG BANG?

*A*ccording to many astronomers, something went "BANG" sixteen billion years ago. The result was the formation of all the billions upon billions of stars and galaxies out in space. Exactly what exploded? Scientists disagree, but they say that, whatever it was, it contained all the "stuff" that the universe is now made of. And, they say that it took billions of years for this to happen.

Scientists can measure many things out in space. There are some amazing machines that they have made to do this. One of them is the famous Hubble Telescope. It can see farther than any other telescope, and it has taken some absolutely beautiful pictures of parts of the universe. If you go outside on a very clear night and look up into the sky, you can see lots of stars, but by far most of them are too far for you to see.

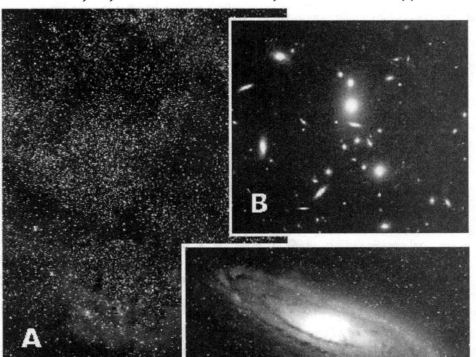

If you were able to look through a telescope, or even a pair of binoculars, you could see FAR more stars than with just your eyes. The sky would look a bit like Picture A, above. There are literally billions and billions of them. It's absolutely fantastic to see!

But, did you know that many of the little points of light that you're seeing are actually not stars at all? Many are galaxies like our own Milky Way. You can see this in Picture B. Each galaxy might look like a single star to our eyes, but each galaxy contains billions more stars. Picture C shows a close-up view of just one of the many millions of galaxies that are in outer space. Scientists have used huge telescopes to look as deep into space as they can, and do you know what they see? More galaxies. More beauty.

Do you think that it's reasonable to say that all of those millions of galaxies containing billions and billions of stars (like our sun) came from an explosion of a little "ball"? Let's ask two basic questions (remember the "science" steps): First, did anybody <u>see</u> this ball, or see it explode? No. Second, if this idea of the ball would be true, it must have been an incredible ball, right? Imagine....it contained <u>all</u> the stuff we now see in our universe. Now, <u>where did the ball come from?</u> Scientists have absolutely no idea! Scientists are guessing about a lot of things out in space. They even argue with each other over the different ideas they all have about how the big bang happened. Let's look at just a few problems with this big bang idea.

A. Explosions don't create order. Have you ever seen something explode? Explosions always ruin things. They cause _disorder_ in things, <u>never _more_</u> order. Can you imagine a tornado ripping through a junkyard and throwing all kinds of scraps of materials into the air? Now, imagine if all

of those pieces that were thrown into the air landed perfectly back on the ground and built, all by accident, a Boeing 747. Could that happen? Of course not, but there are many scientists who say the same about our universe. One such scientist said that it is so complex that it would have required many miracles to get it to the point it is now. We would naturally agree. It's called CREATION!

B. Some galaxies "appear" to be going away from us. For many years, many scientists thought that the reddish color of many of the galaxies means that they are traveling away from us at a high speed. They used this as "proof" of a big explosion. But, other scientists have pointed out that there are many blue-colored galaxies, and they say that this blue color means that those galaxies are coming **toward** us at a high speed. Now, which one is it?

C. As we have seen, God created laws that control forces of nature. One of those laws concerns things that spin. Basically, here is how it works: Imagine a ball that is spinning fast. If there is something attached to the ball that suddenly flies off, that thing will spin in the same direction as the ball from which it came. This is shown at right. If the little ball flew off of the big one while it was spinning, then it too will spin in the same direction.

Many scientists say that the planets of our solar system came from the sun. They say that pieces flew off and started revolving around the sun. Well, if this is true, then all of the planets must be spinning the same way. BUT, Venus, Pluto and Uranus don't! They spin backwards! Also, there are about 60 moons revolving around the planets of this solar system. They should all be spinning the same way if the big bang ideas are true. But, at least 6 of them don't! Why?

D. According to most theories of the big bang, the planets of this solar system came from our sun. If this is true, then all of the planets in this solar system should be made up of the same material. But, they're not. Scientists have now realized that the planets are all very different from each other. Each planet is unique. Some scientists have suggested that the planets formed by some other means, but each time they try to test their theories, they come up far short of what they hoped they would find. Basically, the problem that they have is that there is no way they can explain the existence of our entire solar system.

E. Scientists who believe in the big bang have no idea why large numbers of stars would gather together in galaxies, or why things in the universe spin…things like planets and galaxies. Why do they spin?

There are many more problems with the theory of the big bang, and there are many things about space that completely baffle scientists. They are always looking for answers to their questions. However, many of the answers they come up with are nothing more than new theories!

Some of these questions are very basic ones, too. A good example of one is: Where do stars come from? Most astronomers will agree on this one, but their answer is NOT scientific. They say that clouds of gas CONDENSE in space. That means that the tiny particles of gas pack together very tightly. They say that this eventually becomes very hot and starts burning as a new star. It sounds good until you look at the requirements for knowledge of this type. Do you remember what they are? To have knowledge about this, they must be able to DEMONSTRATE, REPEAT the demonstrations, and both the tests and the results must be OBSERVABLE. So, here are the questions to ask: Have you ever observed gases condensing in space like this? Have you ever seen a new star born, or begin burning?

The answer to both of these questions is NO. Nobody has ever seen a star born! Then why, you might ask, do they tell us that this is how stars form? GOOD QUESTION! Why, indeed? The answer is because it is the only idea that they have. They have no other natural explanation for the birth of stars. To say that stars form this way is unproved, and therefore NOT scientific fact.

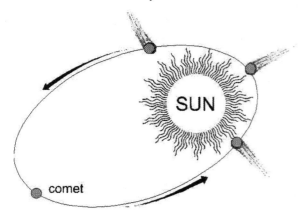

Another question to ask is this: Why are there comets in our solar system? First, what is a comet? A comet is basically a ball of dirty ice that is revolving around the sun in an ELLIPTICAL orbit. That simply means that its path around our sun is sort-of shaped like an egg. Many of the comets we see are called SHORT PERIOD comets. These are comets that go around the sun once in less than 100 years. These comets pass close enough to the sun each time they go around that the sun blows part of the comet apart. The part that is blowing off, or VAPORIZING, looks like a tail, and this tail always aims away from the sun. Once the comet goes farther away from the sun, the tail disappears. But now the comet is smaller, because part of it was blown away. After a while, the comet simply disappears because the sun has vaporized all of it.

The problem for evolutionists is this: Why are there still short period comets? Short period comets can't last more than about 10,000 years. So, if the universe is billions of years old, why are these comets still here? They should have all disappeared billions of years ago. The answer they give, of course, is just a guess. It does not pass the three tests of scientific knowledge. They say that there is a "comet nest" way out in our solar system somewhere, called the Oort Cloud. Every now and then, a new comet leaves this "nest" and starts on its own, new journey. If you ask if this "comet nest" has ever been observed or demonstrated, the answer again is....NO.

What's the point of this? Well, if scientists can't explain things that can be clearly seen – like stars and comets – how can they possibly explain the origin of the whole universe? They can't! Not by natural means, anyway. The existence of the universe, and all of the amazing things found in it, are only explained by SUPERNATURAL means. That means there is a God who created it.

✱ *Now, let's review some of the "big bang" point.*

Fill in the missing word:

1. Many of the points of light that can be seen in space are not single stars, but _____.

2. Explosions don't create _____.

3. According to most evolutionists, the planets of our solar system flew off of the _____.

4. If this was true, then all the planets in the solar system should _____ the same way.

True or false:

5. Galaxies contain billions of stars.   TRUE   FALSE

6. Scientists know what exploded at the time of the "big bang".   TRUE   FALSE

7. At least five planets in our solar system spin the "wrong" way.   TRUE   FALSE

8. The planets in our solar system are each unique.   TRUE   FALSE

9. Scientists know why things in the universe spin.   TRUE   FALSE

10. Scientists have observed stars forming.   TRUE   FALSE

Essay:

Describe why the existence of comets is a problem to evolutionists.

_____

_____

_____

_____

_____

_____

CHEMICALS COME TO LIFE?

*T*he next major step in the development of this planet, according to evolution, was the appearance of life. <u>What is life?</u> The next question is: <u>What became alive?</u>

In order for something to be alive, it must be able to do certain things. Both plants and animals are alive. There are, of course, large differences between them. Plants have no brain, for example. They can't think for themselves. You can't teach a plant to do tricks like you can a dog. But plants do have some of the same abilities that animals have that give them what we call "life".

Virtually all scientists agree that something has life if it can:

1. Ingest nutrients (it can take food into its body, or produce the necessary food to stay alive).
2. Store and use energy, and get rid of wastes.
3. Reproduce (make more of themselves).
4. Grow and move.

Living things are enormously complex. Trying to explain where they came from by accidental, natural processes has become a source of frustration to many scientists. They have come up with several different theories about this. One of the theories is called SPONTANEOUS GENERATION. *Those are big words that simply mean that life just arises by accident from non-living stuff. Many years ago, people used to believe that flies developed from decaying meat, and that rats and mice formed out of piles of old rags. Of course that wasn't true, but most people, and* MOST SCIENTISTS *of that time, believed it. Finally, one scientist proved that the flies were hatching from eggs that female flies were laying on the rotting meat, and that the mice were just using the old rags as nice, warm, cozy homes in which to have their babies.*

Scientists today accept the idea that the only thing OBSERVED and DEMONSTRATED (and therefore scientific) about life, is that <u>life comes from life</u>.

This still doesn't explain how the first living things developed through natural processes. So, some scientists have come up with an idea called PANSPERMIA. *This is another big word that means that somehow some simple living organism flew through space from far, far away, landed on this planet, and started to evolve into all the living things we see today, or that some aliens came and planted life on this planet.* (Do you think this sounds reasonable?)

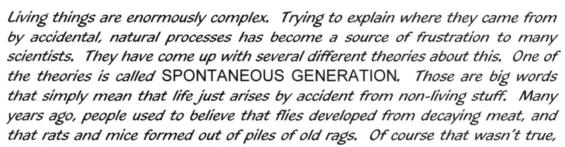

"Hey! Look at that planet back there! Betcha we could start a new life form there, huh?"

Fortunately, most scientists reject this kind of fantasy. It's just a bit too far-fetched to be believable. Besides, it doesn't pass the scientific knowledge tests, either. Even if this were true, it still doesn't explain where life came from. After all, how did the aliens become alive? Where did they come from?

The answer still lies elsewhere. The CURRENT theory (that means, the theory that is held today) is that life began by random chance about 4½ billion years ago when chemicals in the oceans  somehow reacted with each other. This caused some form of early MOLECULES to appear. A molecule is formed when two or more atoms are joined together. These molecules somehow joined with other molecules to make even more complex molecules. This supposedly kept happening until the first, tiny, living cell accidentally formed – and life began!

Of the three theories that scientists have come up with so far, this one seems the most pleasing to most of them. But, again, IT'S JUST AN UNPROVED GUESS! Certainly schools, colleges, television programs and museums do their share in trying to convince people that this is true. The problem is that it DOES NOT PASS THE THREE TESTS OF SCIENCE!

Here is a sample of what many textbooks say about this theory:

"How did life begin on this planet? Experiments have shown that each cell in a living creature comes from a parent cell. If we can trace each cell back to its parent cell, and that cell back to *its* parent cell, and keep doing this back billions of years, we would have to have an original cell at some time. This cell, since it's the original, could not have had a parent cell, could it? Perhaps this original cell came from non-living matter? Most scientists today believe that it did.

People who hold to this theory believe that life might have started under a different set of conditions that they think existed on the earth long ago. No set has been agreed upon by all scientists, and these early life forms can't be found today. But, they outline a series of random, accidental events, which could have led to the origin of living things. Scientists believe that the early earth's atmosphere was very poisonous. It may have contained the exact chemicals needed to form the first molecules

BIOLOGY means "the study of living things".

necessary for life. Some of these molecules might have joined other molecules and possibly become more complex.

Such theories have sparked the imagination of scientists for years, and led them to do many experiments to see if this theory was possible."

Did you note how many times "guess words" were used in the above story? If the story was based on scientific fact, then they would not need to use words like "believe", "assume" and "might have". Let's check it out.

✱ *Highlight the words in the above story that indicate that this is just a guess.*

*N*ow, imagine if you suddenly collapsed from an illness, and you were rushed to the hospital. Imagine that you arrive in the emergency room, and there is a doctor waiting for you. Your parents are frantic because they don't know what's wrong with you. What if the doctor said, "Hmmm. This could be a snake bite......or maybe a bike crash? Uh, this might be a case of malaria." Would your parents be satisfied with the doctor if he said this? Of course not! You would expect that the doctor would know more than that! If he **did** say that, he certainly would not be a doctor there for too long.

What would you think of a scientist who used words like that when describing a theory, and then told you that his theory is a fact?

Let's go back for a minute to look a bit closer at this idea that somehow chemicals combined to accidentally form life. Do you remember the lesson on the big bang? Do you remember the drawing of a Boeing 747 jumbo jet being built all by chance from things that a tornado picks up and drops? Well, the same idea applies here. Living things are incredibly complex. Chance and accident don't build them. Even if the story of life accidentally forming in the ocean as a tiny cell were true, that tiny cell would have been VERY complex. How complex would it be? Well, imagine this: Scientists estimate that you have between 50 to 100 *trillion* cells in your body. That number looks like this:

100,000,000,000,000

That number is so high that it baffles the mind. But, scientists know that EACH CELL is just as complex as an entire city, like Philadelphia. Imagine that! Imagine all the many things that go on inside a city that size. All the office buildings, the cars and trucks, the phone lines, the computers, the plumbing, etc. Each cell, as tiny as it is, is just as complex inside as a city. And, each cell has all the information in it to be any other cell in your body! Think about that for a minute! If the cell in your eye has the information to be a cell in a knee cap or a fingernail, why aren't they using that information? Why are eye cells eye cells? Why are skin cells skin cells? Why are your muscle cells not using the information they have to be hair cells?

The answer is DESIGN. Each cell knows which information to shut off. The cells in your eye have shut off the information on how to be a kneecap or a toenail. But, how? Design! God has placed a special code in all living things (called DNA), and this code tells all the cells exactly how to act and what to be. Accident and evolution can NEVER explain how all this amazing beauty and complexity came about. Nor can it explain how this information is energized and becomes life!

The only thing EVER observed about the origin of life is: **LIFE COMES FROM LIFE.**

Did you know that if your whole DNA code were to be written down, it would fill over *1,000 books with 500 pages each* – each book the same size as an encyclopedia volume?

SIMPLE LIFE BECOMES COMPLEX? (PART 1)

*A*ccording to evolution, the tiny, simple cell in the ocean 4½ billion years ago became you and me. How did that supposedly happen? Do you remember the fairy tale of the beautiful princess who kissed a frog? Do you remember what happened to the frog? It turned into a handsome, young prince. Then, the two of them got married and lived happily ever after.

Sounds good! I'd be happy if I could kiss a stone and have it turn into a $100 bill. But that can't happen, of course. Or......could it? What if I kissed the stone for a long time? What if I could live for a million years and kept kissing the stone for that long? Would it turn into money if I add a lot of time? Could the frog somehow eventually turn into a prince if it was given millions of years?

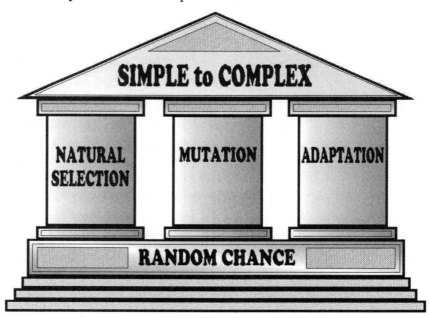

The answer, of course, is NO. You would need a miracle. The same is true about the tiny cell turning into a human. It would take a miracle. Interestingly, evolutionists seem to believe in that type of miracle, but not one in which God (or even anything supernatural) made life on earth. So how do evolutionists say that the cell became you and me? How did the simple become complex? Here's the "recipe":

1. You need lots and lots of time – billions of years for this recipe to work.

2. You need lots and lots of "accidents" – good accidents, though. You need the kind of accidents that make things better and more complex. (Hint: Have you EVER seen an accident that makes things better and more complex?)

3. You need nature on your side. Nature needs to weed out things that you no longer need, and develop things that you *do* need. In some cases along the way, nature will have to accidentally develop things that you don't need now, but WILL need in the future. Nature will, in these cases, have to "think ahead" to develop parts of your body that will be suited for the next stage of evolution.

4. You need <u>lots and lots of imagination, and a good deal of faith</u> that your recipe can work!

SIMPLE to COMPLEX

NATURAL SELECTION | MUTATION | ADAPTATION

RANDOM CHANCE

Let's look at the recipe the evolutionists say caused this jump from the tiny cell to you and me — simple to complex. You'll notice that the first pillar in this temple is called "natural selection". That means that nature itself determined what would evolve (change into something more complex). Charles Darwin used this term to try to show that, as a creature was evolving (growing more complex through small changes), nature would weed out the changes that were "bad" (or something that the creature can't use), and keep only the things that were "good" to help the creature survive. This assumes at least two things: 1) That more complex parts were being added to the creature somehow, and 2) That nature somehow "knew" what would be beneficial for the creature to evolve to the next step. Both are false, and anyway, have NEVER been observed.

Part of natural selection is an idea called "survival of the fittest". This is a term that has been used for a long time by evolutionists to try to show how various creatures were SELECTED, or chosen, by nature to eventually become something new. But, does nature select things to evolve?

Natural Selection: Survival of the Fittest…..

Again, the idea that nature selects things <u>to evolve</u> has NEVER BEEN OBSERVED. It is one of the things that evolutionists have to accept by faith. Natural selection is a fact of life, but let's look at what <u>IS</u> observed when we talk about "survival of the fittest". Here's a story from my past….

I used to live in Africa and I worked in a large game reserve where there were lots of animals. One day, we were driving along a road in the game reserve, and we came across a lioness that was just sitting under a tree in the heat of the day. She didn't look interested in anything, and she was too far away from us to get a good picture. We were about to leave when we saw some warthogs coming up from a waterhole on the opposite side of the road. Way behind the main group of warthogs was another one who was obviously lame. He was limping far behind the others. As the warthogs crossed the road behind our car, they came into full view of the lioness, but she showed no interest in trying to catch one for a meal. But, a minute later, the lame one appeared into her view. The lioness immediately knew by instinct that this warthog would be easy to catch, because she could see that it was limping. She crept into the long grass and disappeared from our view. Seconds later, however, she burst out of her cover and was able to catch the warthog without any trouble.

This type of thing goes on in nature ALL THE TIME. But, what do you observe about this story? Which warthog was caught? The lame one. The healthy ones survived. In nature, it's normally the lame, the weak, the sick, the old, the young, etc. who are caught by the predators. What happened to the other warthogs? Did their offspring start becoming birds or elephants? No, that's not what is observed. The only thing observed is that they survived. If nothing happens to them, they will be observed to make baby warthogs — nothing else!

It's plain to see here that the ONLY thing observed about "survival of the fittest" is simply that the fittest survive. The evolutionists believe that the healthy and strong ones were somehow able to change into another kind of animal. But, that's not scientific, is it? It's NEVER been observed or demonstrated. That idea has to be accepted by faith. Natural selection does work in nature, but only to help creatures survive — not to turn them into another kind.

An interesting story: In a natural history museum in Washington D.C., there was an exhibit that attempted to illustrate natural selection. It showed a crayfish-like creature (supposedly our ancestor) coming out of the sea and onto dry land. The exhibit told of the problem, because the crayfish creature couldn't breathe on land. It needed to stay in the water to survive. So, how was our "ancestor" able to make this transition from water to air? Well, they explained that "perhaps" very long ago one of these creatures developed a lucky "pre-adaptation". They called this lucky pre-adaptation a "proto-lung". In other words, by chance a blob of tissue developed in one of these creatures that, *amazingly*, over a long time, generation after generation, became a usable lung that eventually helped the creature to adapt once it crawled out of the water!

Cute story, but *pure fantasy!* First, this type of incredible, chance accident could *never* happen in the real world – only in people's minds. Second, if this had actually happened, natural selection would have weeded out the "proto-lung" simply because it's tissue that the creature CANNOT USE while it's living in the water. Therefore, according to natural selection, this tissue would have been considered "bad" because it's using up resources that are needed by the creature elsewhere. Natural selection is well understood, but it does NOT support Darwinian evolution.

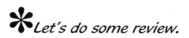 *Let's do some review.*

True or false:

1. Scientists during medieval times used to believe that flies came from garbage.   TRUE   FALSE

2. "Panspermia" is the theory that life somehow came from outer space.   TRUE   FALSE

3. Evolutionists today believe that life came about by chance about 4½ billion years ago.

     TRUE   FALSE

4. "Biology" is the study of fossils.   TRUE   FALSE

5. The special code in all living things is called DNA.   TRUE   FALSE

6. Scientists have observed living things forming from non-living things.   TRUE   FALSE

7. "Natural selection" is an observed fact of life.   TRUE   FALSE

8. "Survival of the fittest" is a part of "natural selection".   TRUE   FALSE

Fill in the missing words:

9. For something to be alive, it must be able to:

   a. _____

   b. _____

   c. _____

   d. _____

10. The only thing observed about "survival of the fittest" is that _____

SIMPLE LIFE BECOMES COMPLEX? (PART 2)

Mutations.....

*E*volutionists say that it wasn't natural selection on its own that produced evolving creatures. They say that there are other parts to the recipe. You'll notice that the next pillar is called MUTATIONS. What is a mutation? We're going to greatly simplify this so you can better understand what this is. We're going to start by looking at the DNA code.

Do you have any tinker toys? If you do, you might want to get some that match these three at the right at this time. We're just going to use three pieces. You know what the alphabet is. The alphabet contains letters. The letters are like a code for making words. If you put letters together in a meaningful way, you can make words. Words alone don't say much, but if you put words into sentences, you can communicate a great many thoughts and ideas to other people. But, suppose you wanted to write a letter to someone, but you were only allowed to use nine of the letters in the alphabet. You really couldn't write much, could you? To illustrate this, let's use the three pieces of tinker toy and see how many letters of the alphabet you can make.

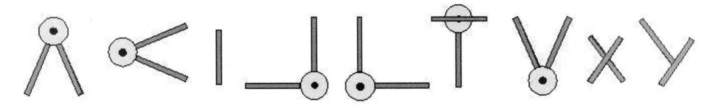

If you put the three pieces together in the right way, you can make **A, C, I, J, L, T, V, X & Y.** That's only nine letters. How many words can you make with those nine letters? Very few, right? What would you need to do in order to make more letters of the alphabet? <u>You would have to add more tinker toy parts, of course.</u> And, if you add the right ones, you could make all the letters in the alphabet, and then you could make all the words that there are.

It's the same with ALL living things. Every living thing is made up of a special code, too. This code is called DNA. DNA is sort-of like the letters in the alphabet. Your DNA code is a molecule that is found in each of the cells of your body, and it determines all the things that make you who you are physically. It determines the color of your eyes and hair, the shape of your nose, how tall you will be, what your voice sounds like, etc. It's absolutely amazing! It's like having your very own alphabet.

The tiny cell that evolutionists say started billions of years ago would have had a DNA code, too. Its code would have been very complex, but it would have been MUCH simpler than the code that makes up you and me. You and I have eyes, ears, hands and feet, and MANY other parts that the

first, tiny, simple cell would <u>not</u> have had. Each of the parts of your body has a special part of the DNA code all its own. Now, suppose you wanted to grow wings so you could fly. What would need to happen to your DNA code? The same thing as the alphabet we just looked at. If you want to make more letters of the alphabet so you could make more words and sentences, you need to add more tinker toy parts. Well, if you want to grow wings, you have to add more special code to your DNA – VERY complex "wing-growing" code!

But, there is a HUGE problem. This CANNOT happen. It has NEVER been observed in the past and it is NOT being observed today that in nature new code can be added to what is already there. Many scientists recognize this as a HUGE problem for the theory of evolution. The first, tiny cell would have needed to add MANY, MANY new parts to its code to become you and me, BUT THIS IS IMPOSSIBLE, and it has never been observed!

So, how do they say it happened? Here's where we get back to the idea of MUTATIONS. <u>A mutation is something that has gone wrong with the DNA code.</u> Somehow, the DNA code was damaged, or copied wrongly as the cells were dividing. To understand this, let's go back to the tinker toys. Look at the letter below in Figure 1 at the left. It's a capital **G**. Now, what if we were copying that letter many times very fast, and we made a mistake and caused some damage so that one of the letters looked like the letter in Figure 2? There's definitely something wrong with it. Or, what if part of the **G** was copied too many times, so that one of them looked like the one in Figure 3? We would call these MUTATIONS. Something has gone wrong with the code. In living things, mutations are very often harmful or deadly to the creature. Even if a creature has a mutation that is not harmful or deadly, the mutation has NEVER been observed to make the creature more complex.

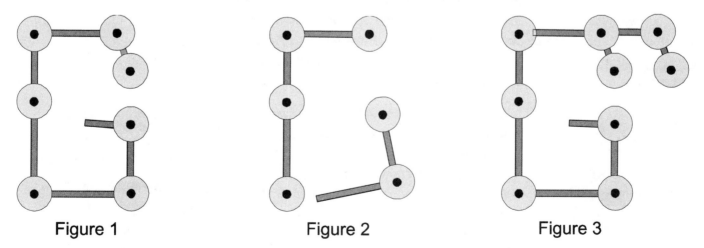

| Figure 1 | Figure 2 | Figure 3 |

But, notice something very important! In both Figure 2 and Figure 3, no new parts were added to what was originally found in the letter in Figure 1. All the parts are the same.

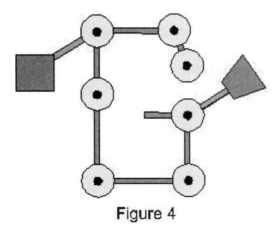

Figure 4

But, look now at Figure 4, at left. You can notice two more shapes that were not part of the original capital **G**. *How did these new shapes get there? I simply added them to the Figure 1 drawing. Now, figure 4 is more complex than Figure 1. It's now potentially becoming a brand new letter, one never seen before.*

This is the type of thing that evolutionists say happened to the first living cell. More useful "parts" (or information) were added to the DNA code of the cell to make it more complex. And, if this was true, it must have happened millions and millions of times to form into you and me. But, how? The evolutionists say it was mutations that did it.

NOTE: This is not true! No mutation in nature has ever been observed to add more useful parts, or complexity, to the DNA code. All living things start with a code. This code can be damaged, or part of it can be destroyed or removed, or the parts can be moved around in different ways. But, NO NEW INFORMATION CAN BE ADDED IN NATURE!

NOTE: Even if scientists are somehow able to take code from one creature and "patch" it into the code of another, you're still left with the very same question: Where did the complex code come from originally?

A SERIOUS PROBLEM: Most mutations are harmful or deadly. So, even if there was an occasional mutation among them that *somehow* made creatures more complex, then imagine the billions of harmful or deadly mutations that "evolving creatures" were *somehow* able to avoid! Impossible!

An interesting question about mutations...

Can a mutation ever produce a good result or ever benefit a living thing, or help it in some way?

The answer depends on what "good" and "benefit" mean. Mutations can sometimes produce conditions in, or for, a living creature that might seem good, or beneficial. Let's take a look at two examples, and then we'll see what really happened. We will see that these examples of "good" mutations are actually proof that mutations work AGAINST Darwinian evolution.

First, let's consider malaria. Malaria is a terrible disease that is often found in tropical areas of the world, and is carried by mosquitos. Many people die from malaria. But, there are some people in Africa who can be bitten by a malaria-carrying mosquito and NOT get the disease. Why? The answer can be found in their blood. Some members of various tribes of Africans have a mutation that helps to block malaria. That certainly sounds like a good thing, right? Some evolutionists like to point to this mutation as a good example of evidence for evolution.

But, there is a big problem. This blood mutation is called SICKLE-CELL ANEMIA. When a child in these tribes receives this blood disorder from both of his parents, HE DIES! In these tribes, at least one person out of every four dies from the mutation! That's more than normally would die from malaria! Is this a "good" thing? Certainly not. No doctor alive thinks it is, either. So, while this mutation might have a certain benefit in blocking malaria, it does NOT add more information to the DNA code. It only shows that there is something wrong with it. (By the way, if this is such a "good" mutation, shouldn't everyone try to get it?)

Another example…

Let's imagine that there is an island in the Pacific Ocean where a certain kind of beetle lives. These beetles can fly. But, a mutation occurs in one of them that damages the DNA code for flight so that the beetle does not have the ability to grow wings. Now, if this is the type of mutation that can be passed on to the next generations, then all of the beetle's offspring have the damaged code as well. None of them can fly. The mutation is then passed down to all the next generations of that kind of beetle, so that after a while, there are two types of beetles on the island – ones that can fly, and ones that can't.

Now, a big hurricane comes through. The winds are terrible. The beetles are all frightened, and so they do what comes naturally to them by instinct – they open their wings to fly away from the problem. All of the ones that fly are blown into the sea and are drowned. The ones that can't scurry under rocks or anything they find for shelter. Soon, after several storms like this, all of the ones that could fly are dead. Only the flightless ones are left.

Couldn't we say that this mutation was a "good" one? It certainly helped the beetle to survive. If the mutation had never happened, then all of the beetles would have drowned, right? Yes, that's true, BUT…. remember that now information is gone. Permanently! The DNA information for flight is gone forever. Information has been lost.

Here's the problem: Evolution requires the opposite! *Evolution needs information to be ADDED, not removed! So, even though this mutation helped the beetle to survive, it did the opposite of what Darwinian evolution needs.*

Adaptation…..

Finally, evolutionists say that creatures became more complex through ADAPTATION. This simply means that they were able to change their bodies somehow so that they could live in different environments.

> Oh, hey…WOW! It sure feels good to have finally evolved lungs to breathe out here!

One example of this that is used in museums is the idea that creatures in the sea were somehow able to ADAPT to living on land. Since evolutionists say that life began in the water, somehow some early life form, as it was evolving, was able to come out of the water and start living in air on land. They have to say this because you and I, and many other creatures, live on land. But, if they are going to say this, they must show us <u>how</u> this happened. Again, their answer is that many good, information-adding mutations caused these sea creatures to evolve lungs so that they could adapt to life out of water. (The simple, observable truth is that a creature that lives in water, like a fish, would be dead in just a few minutes if it came out on dry land!)

Again, we have to go back to science and ask the three questions. Has something like this ever been observed? NO. Has anyone done experiments that show how this could have happened in nature? NO. Are there creatures in the fossil record that had a half-gill (like a fish) and a half-lung (like birds and mammals)? NO. This is just an assumption on the part of the evolutionists.

There are, of course, true adaptations in nature. Some creatures are able to change to live in surrounding conditions. But this is because God has created in their DNA code the ability to do this. The creature that's adapting to a new environment still stays the same kind of creature that it and all of its ancestors have always been. But if it's able to adapt to a new environment, it's because part of its DNA code allows its body to change in some small way (an example of MICROEVOLUTION – page vii), and it might not have needed that part of its DNA code before. God simply did this to help the creature survive in a wider array of environments.

Charles Darwin saw this happening in finches he was studying on the Galapagos Islands. He noticed that the finches on one of the islands were slightly different than those on another island. And those differed slightly from finches on yet another island. And they all were slightly different than the finches on the mainland. He supposed that this was proof that the finches were evolving. He thought that if small changes like this could keep happening, then eventually the creature would become a new kind of bird or animal.

But, what was Charles Darwin really seeing? He was only seeing small changes <u>within a kind</u>. The finches were ALL finches. They stayed finches. They had always been finches. They will always be finches. They never turned into anything else. They never said "meow".

The important thing to remember about adaptations is that the creature that's adapting STAYS THE SAME KIND OF CREATURE. A finch does not become an eagle just because it was able to adapt in some way. A fish does not become a lizard because it was able to adapt in some way. But, evolution requires that the creature eventually becomes another kind of creature. This is wrong, and again, has NEVER been observed.

✱Let's do a quick review.

Fill in the missing word:

1. _____ is the special "life code" that all living things have.

2. Damaged DNA, or a mistake in the copying of DNA, is called a _____

3. Evolutionists say that mutations must have caused living things to become _____

4. Mutations have never been _____ to add more complexity to DNA code.

5. Creatures that can adapt, and even change slightly in appearance, always stay the same _____ of creature. They never turn into anything else.

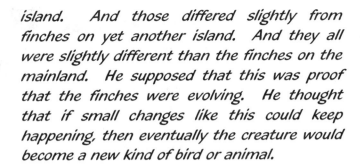

HOW OLD IS THE EARTH?

*A*ccording to evolution, life has been evolving on the earth for 4½ billion years, so they would say that the earth itself is even older than that. They have to say that because, according to the recipe for evolving life, it would take many hundreds of millions of years. But is there any solid, scientific evidence that the earth is this old? The answer is NO. Some scientists have come up with different methods to try to prove that the earth is this old, but the tests are very inaccurate.

What if scientists discovered solid evidence that the earth is actually only several thousands of years old? What would that do to the theory of evolution? It would make it impossible, of course, because the "recipe" for evolution requires many millions of years. So, scientists who believe evolution must defend, in any way they can, the idea that the earth is very, very old.

But, what does the evidence say? Even though we cannot prove how old the earth is by science, there are other ways to estimate it. The most important way is to go back to the Word of God, the Bible, to see what it says. There we can read that God made the earth and everything in it, on it, and over it, in six days. Adam was made on the sixth day. Then, the Bible tells us how old Adam was when his son, Seth, was born and how old Seth was when his son was born, and so on. Do you remember this chart from an earlier lesson? Let's look at it again.

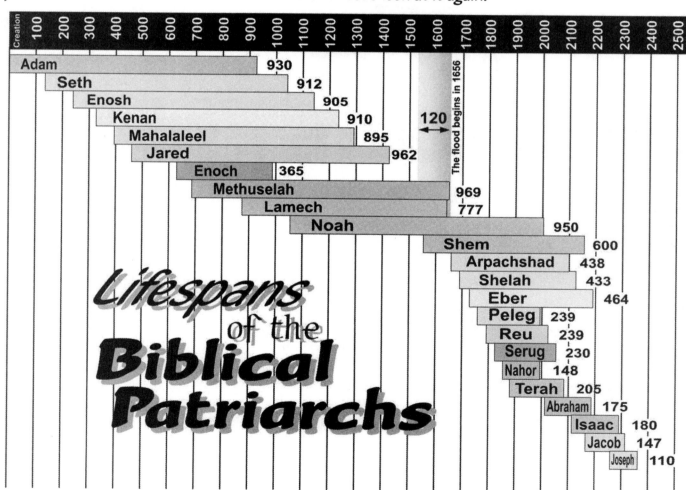

Looking at this chart, you can see that from the time Adam was created to the time Joseph died was over 2350 years. In the New Testament book of Matthew there is another list of genealogies (names) from Abraham through King David the whole way down to Jesus Christ. In the Old Testament books of I and II Chronicles, we can fairly accurately see how many years it was from King David to Jesus. We know that Jesus was born about 2000 years ago. So, if we add up all of these years together, we can see that the time from the creation of Adam to today is around

6,000 years, perhaps a little more. Very few people who believe the Bible will argue with this. It's actually quite clear.

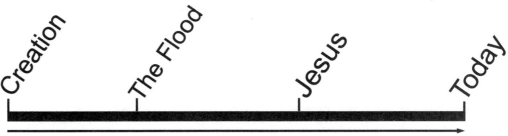

about 6000 years

The problem comes when people try to reinterpret the days of creation from the first day up to Adam as billions of years. As we have already seen, these were literal days – not billions of years. Of course, evolutionists don't believe the Bible (or at least, believe the Genesis account literally), and they say that evolution must have happened extremely slowly. That's why they MUST say the earth is billions of years old.

What do evolutionists use to prove their idea of the great age of the earth? They try to test rocks with methods they have developed that will supposedly give the age of the rocks they test. They are very happy with some of the results they get, and these are the results that are published in many textbooks, talked about on TV programs, and used in museum displays. But, there is a problem with these tests – THE CONCLUSIONS AREN'T SCIENTIFIC.

One of the reasons for this is that evolutionists ASSUME things about the earth, and the tests are based on these ASSUMPTIONS. To assume something means that you suppose it to be true, but you don't know it for a fact. One of these assumptions is that "the present is the key to the past". They say that processes that shaped the earth are working today just as they did millions and billions of years ago. But, this is not science – it is not knowledge. This is just an idea that is not provable since nobody was alive then to observe it.

To illustrate this, imagine that someone took you into a room with nothing in it but a burning candle. The person then asks you, "How long has it been since this candle was first lit?" Could you answer correctly? No, you could not. Here are 3 reasons why:

1. You do not know if the wax is a fast-burning wax or a slow-burning wax.
2. You do not know how long the candle was when it was new. Was it a 3-foot long candle, or a 9-inch long candle?
3. You do not know if there was ever a time when the candle might have been blown out, and then relit at some later time.

All you can do is guess, or assume when the candle was first lit. But, you cannot know. This is true with the special tests the scientists do when trying to date the rocks. There are many things they cannot know. But, there are also other things some scientists do with these tests.

When scientists do these tests on rocks, they do several, or many tests on samples of the rock they are trying to date. But, many of these tests give *VERY DIFFERENT DATES* for the same rock! How could that be? Do you think that maybe there might be something wrong with the test itself? Even so, how do scientists know which date they want to believe? Which date is correct in their view? They simply go back to the

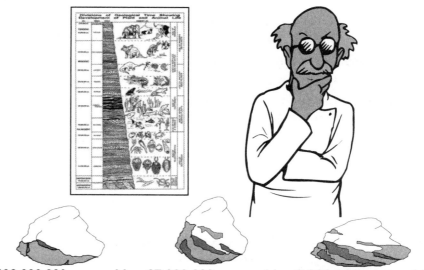

192,000,000 years old   67,000,000 years old   9,000,000 years old

geological column chart to see where they think it should fit in. If a rock contains fossils, then it's even easier. They see what fossil animal it is, find that type of creature on the chart, note the date that the fossilized creature supposedly lived, then choose the experiment with the date closest to that! So, what they are doing is choosing the date closest to what *THEY THINK* it should be.

That brings up another question: What about the other experiments that showed different dates? The scientist simply says that those samples were probably contaminated, so that's why the experiment showed a "wrong" date. Well, if that's true, how do they know that the experiment they chose to believe wasn't the one contaminated?

> Do you see what's going on here? Many scientists simply believe evidence that is very questionable. They really don't know which one is correct – they just choose to believe the one **they want.**

Is there any REAL scientific evidence of the earth's age?...

There are quite a number of features about the earth, the moon, the solar system, the universe, and some living things on the earth that indicate an age quite different from the ones the evolutionists believe. Here are just a few you might find interesting:

- Do you remember the lesson on the big bang? One of the interesting things we looked at was the existence of comets. If our solar system was billions of years old, there should be no more short period comets. They should have all disappeared billions of years ago. But, we still have lots of comets. Why? The most reasonable explanation is that the solar system is not that old!

- Earth's close "buddy" out in space is the moon. The moon revolves around the earth. But, this close neighbor of ours is slowly **RECEDING**. That means it is slowly going away from the earth. Scientists can measure how fast it is moving away. They have figured out something interesting: If the moon started out more or less where it is today, and if it has been receding at the same rate as it is today, and if the universe is billions of years old, then the moon should be far out of sight by now! But, it's not. Why? Perhaps the solar system is much younger than the evolutionists say it is! There are other fascinating features about the moon that indicate that it is far younger than evolutionists believe.

- People get oil by drilling deep into the earth. When they get to the oil, it always gushes out. That's because it is under lots of pressure. This confuses people who believe in evolution. Why? Because if the earth was millions of years old, the pressure should not be there any more, or at least, it should be much less than it is now because the pressure would have forced the oil to leak out through the rocks. So, why is there still so much pressure down there? The probable answer is that it hasn't been down there very long - perhaps just thousands of years.

- How about things on the earth itself?
    1. Niagara Falls is wearing away the rocks beneath it at a known rate. If you calculate back in time at the same rate, you will find that the falls started about 4-5 thousand years ago.
    2. The Mississippi Delta has been building up slowly at a rate known to scientists. If they apply this rate back to the original place where the delta started, it appears to be about 4-5 thousand years old.

    3. The oldest known living things on the earth are the bristlecone pine trees. How old are they? About 4 thousand years old.

Do you notice the age of these items? Their ages are all estimated to be about the same. There are other interesting features of the earth that date to about this age, too. Can you think of any reason why? How long ago did the flood end?

A fascinating story...

During World War II, six P-38 fighter planes were traveling with some others over Greenland to join the war in England. They ran into bad weather and were forced to land on the ice because they ran out of fuel. Before they landed, they radioed their position so that they could be rescued. Nine days later, they were found and taken to safety, but the planes all had to be abandoned on the ice. This happened in July, 1942.

In 1988, just 46 years later, a team who was searching for the planes to restore them found the whole squadron. They thought they would be able to just brush the snow off the wings, fix them up, put some fuel in them and fly them away. What they found, however, baffled everyone.

The planes were all 250 feet below the ice!! Scientists had always told us that it would take huge amounts of time to build up ice that thick. They were wrong. The snow had compacted and built up in less than 50 years over these planes. This is evidence that some things don't need to take as long as evolutionists think.

Remember that science is a process — a process used to answer questions, or to solve problems. The main question that evolutionists must find an answer for (and one of the major problems they must solve) is this: *Where did complex living things come from?* This is really two questions: 1. What is life and how did it appear? and 2. Where did complexity come from? Furthermore, they *must* answer these questions according to the rules of science.

There is no evolutionary answer for the first question. Do you think that they've found the solution to the second? Do you think that they've answered the question according to the rules of science? Is their theory based more on faith and wishful thinking, or do you think it's scientific fact?

❋ *Let's review what we've learned about the age of Earth.*

True or false:

1. All scientists are always objective. They are only concerned with truth.   TRUE   FALSE

2. In order for evolution to work, scientists MUST say the earth is very old.   TRUE   FALSE

3. The Bible indicates that the earth is billions of years old.   TRUE   FALSE

4. Evolutionists test the rocks for their age using methods that don't assume anything.

   TRUE   FALSE

5. Age tests on samples of the same rock always give the same age.   TRUE   FALSE

6. Scientists sometimes just assume things.   TRUE   FALSE

7. The fact that the moon is slowly receding from the earth can give us a clue to its age.

   TRUE   FALSE

8. Oil pressure deep in the earth causes a big problem for the "creation model".   TRUE   FALSE

9. Niagara Falls, the Mississippi Delta, and bristlecone pine trees are just some of the examples we can

   look at that suggest the age of the earth since the flood.   TRUE   FALSE

10. In very cold regions of the world, ice takes many thousands of years to build up.

   TRUE   FALSE

EVOLUTION: ODDS & ENDS

In this unit, we have looked very briefly at the basic problems with the main "pillars" of evolution. But there are far more problems that evolution faces. The origin of some things is completely unexplainable. In other cases, evolutionists have looked at observable things and have become excited because they think they see evolution happening. But they don't. Let's consider a few examples of each. We'll start with an evolutionary favorite – the peppered moth.

Evolutionists have used the story of the peppered moth for years to show how evolution works through natural selection. The story goes something like this:

The peppered moth is found in two basic forms – light and dark. Many years ago, before the Industrial Revolution in England, the dark ones were rare because when they sat on the light-colored trees they stood out much more than the light-colored ones, and so they were easy to spot by the birds that liked to eat them. However, during the Industrial Revolution the trees began to get dark because of pollution from nearby factories. Now the lighter moths were easier to see because they stood out against the dark background, so they began to get eaten while the dark ones became more numerous. Later on, when the pollution was cleaned up, the trees began to get lighter again and so the darker moths began to be seen easier. So, they diminished in number because of the birds, while the lighter ones became more numerous again because they were harder to see now against the lighter trees. These shifts in populations were well documented. Birds were filmed eating these moths off of the trees.

Does this story give us a good example of evolution in action? ABSOLUTELY NOT! It does show how natural selection can work, but it shows no evolution happening at all. The peppered moths are still peppered moths. Even if this went on for many millions of years, there is still no way that the moth can become more complex and change into another type of creature.

But, the story doesn't end there. It was discovered that peppered moths don't even rest on trees during the day! Scientists still don't know where they rest. So, what about the photographs of birds eating them off the trees? Well, it seems that the darker side of human nature was at work again here. The photographs were faked! The moths used in the pictures were ones that were bred in a laboratory, and then placed on the trees by the very people doing the photography! In some cases, dead moths were glued to the trees so that the birds could be filmed eating them!

Thankfully, even many evolutionists are throwing out this whole story. They realize that it just doesn't prove anything they had hoped it would, and that the "evidence" is false. Unfortunately, many millions of students around the world don't know this. They still are taught that the peppered moth story is good evidence for evolution.

Then there's the story of the horse. For a long time evolutionists showed a detailed series of fossils of horse toe bones and claimed that these clearly showed evolutionary steps in the development of the horse. Many museums built beautiful displays showing these bones along with a painting of each of the creatures. It looked very convincing.

But again, let's see what really is going on with these exhibits. The first of the "evolutionary horses" is called EOHIPPUS or, the "dawn horse". This little creature turned out to be nothing more than a hyrax, or rock rabbit. They still exist in many places of the world today. The other fossils are all from horses. There are many species of horse today. Some are very small; others are very large. But, they are all just horses. Horses breed horses and nothing else.

Most museums have removed the exhibits of horse evolution because they now know that the evidence is just not there like they once thought. Here is another reason why: As fossils have been removed from the ground, it was discovered that some of the older horses (on the evolution scale) were buried ABOVE the younger ones. How could that be? According to evolution, that would mean that they're YOUNGER. In other places, fossils from several of the supposed evolutionary links were found buried together. That would mean that all those evolutionary horse links lived at the same time.

There are other problems with horse evolution, too. Now they have had to rewrite their story of the horse to try to be consistent with the facts. The new stories aren't any better because they still assume that horses evolved. But, of course, there is no evidence.

The problems continue. Consider, for example, the origin of whales. Where do they come from? The Bible teaches simply that God made them on the fifth day of creation with all of the other creatures of the sea. The evolutionary answer has to be much more complicated and confusing. The reason is not hard to understand. You see, whales are mammals, and as such, they are very different from fish, even though they might look similar in many ways to fish.

What is a mammal? An animal is considered a mammal if it is a VERTEBRATE (has a spinal column), is warm-blooded, and feeds its young milk through special glands. (Most scientists also say that mammals usually have hair and give birth to live babies.)

So what's the problem that evolution has with whales? Well, for the most part, mammals live on land. The evolutionists have a hard-enough time trying to explain how mammals developed from creatures that originally came from the sea. Such creatures don't have lungs; they breathe in a completely different way. Fish get oxygen from the water through special organs called gills. Gills are very different from lungs. Lungs remove oxygen from air.

Now, here's where it begins to get interesting. How does a gill turn into a lung? Or, how does a gill completely disappear while lungs begin to develop? The answer is — THEY DON'T! And, by the way, there are no fossils showing any creature that had a half-gill, half lung. But, the problem with whales is that, according to evolution, mammals developed over millions of years on land. How is it that we have great animals in the sea that look like fish, but are mammals?

Some evolutionists have tried to tackle this problem. Some of their answers seem very funny, but at the same time, sad, because they mislead many people into believing yet another lie. Here's what some evolutionists believe and teach:

Many millions of years ago, long after mammals had fully developed on land, there was a type of black wolf that lived near the edge of the sea. This creature learned to like fish, so he spent much time jumping into the water to catch them. After quite a while doing this, the wolf-like creature began to swim out farther into the waves after its food. It spent more and more time in the ocean. Over millions of years, its front legs began to turn into fins. It completely lost its back legs, and its tail area grew into a large "flipper". To breathe properly, its nose began to evolve from the front of his head up to the top and just turned into a hole. His skin changed, too, to have the special blubber that whales have to keep them insulated. These, and many other changes, all by chance, eventually turned the wolf-like dog into the whale we have today.

Well, how does that sound? If you don't like that idea, perhaps you might like the story that other evolutionists tell. They say that it wasn't a wolf-like creature that turned into a whale, but a cow-like creature! So, it seems you have a choice -- either a wolf or a cow turned into a whale!

What about flowering plants? Where did they come from? Do you know that Charles Darwin himself wrestled with this idea? He called it "that abominable mystery". That's not surprising! Of course it's a mystery to evolutionists; they have no choice but to guess and use their imaginations! But, people who believe the Bible don't have to guess. The Bible states that God made them, in all their vast, beautiful array, on the third day of creation.

But, let's get back to the evolutionists. Few have tried to tackle this problem. The ones that have tried have come up with some of the most incredible stories yet! One evolutionist believes that flowering plants were invented by dinosaurs. That's right, DINOSAURS! Of course, he doesn't offer a scientific (or even realistic) explanation of exactly how the dinosaurs accomplished this.

But, he's not alone in trying to solve the problem. Another evolutionist claimed that insects were evolving at the same time that the flowers were developing. His story goes something like this:

Insects were looking for food, and so they discovered pollen. At first they began to eat that. However, the plants apparently didn't want them eating the pollen, so they developed a substitute food – nectar! At the same time, the plants began making their flowers more desirable to the insects. They made attractive smells, colors, and patterns to help guide the insects in to the nectar.

Does any of this sound like a scientific explanation for the origin of flowering plants? <u>Does it even sound reasonable?</u> Of course not, but when you have to defend a theory, when there's no scientific evidence for it, what other choice do you have?

Here's another puzzler for evolutionists: Where did male and female come from? The Bible states that God is the one who made male and female. But, if you try to explain it through accident and chance, you're forced to come up with strange stories again. And, if you're going to try to say that the stories are scientific, well....you know what would be required for that - hard evidence and repeatable experiments.

It is easy to tell the difference between the male and female of many creatures on the earth. With others, it is a bit harder. Yet still with others, it is impossible to see the difference, like with certain kinds of parrots. You need to take blood or other types of body tissue samples and have them analyzed in a laboratory to be able to tell if it's a male or a female. Yet, they themselves can tell the difference easily and immediately!

It's impossible enough to explain scientifically how creatures evolved. How then can the rise of GENDER (male or female) be explained by evolution? How did creatures reproduce before there was male and female? If there were only a male of a "newly-evolving" creature, it would be impossible for that creature to reproduce without a female. That creature would immediately become extinct when he dies. Also, there are many important differences between male and female. How did these differences, which perfectly help to make a complete match between the two creatures, develop all by chance — AND at the same time?!

Let's consider one more of the many problems that evolutionists have to face. If evolution actually happened, then there should be "vestiges" of the past. That means, there should be evidence, within our bodies (and within the bodies of all creatures), of organs or parts of organs that are no longer needed. They are disappearing because we no longer need them as we continue to evolve. If there were such organs, they would be evidence that evolution perhaps actually happened. These would be known as VESTIGIAL ORGANS.

Well, for years evolutionists have taught that there are, in fact, many vestigial organs. At one time, they believed that there were well over one hundred such organs in the human body. They taught that there was no use for these (no function any more), and so they must be leftovers from our evolutionary past! One example of this was the appendix. Since they knew of no current function for this organ, they assumed it had none, and was evidence of evolution.

Now, however, scientists in the medical field have discovered at least some function for ALL these organs. They are all important in some way or another. They all serve a purpose. Most scientists now accept that there are no vestigial organs. That is evidence against evolution.

One other interesting question that evolution can't answer: What is life, itself? Imagine that, by some sheer strokes of "brilliant" accidents, the DNA molecule did somehow evolve. There it sits, in all of its enormous complexity. The point now is.......SO WHAT?! You still don't have life! The DNA molecule can't do anything on its own. It needs something to guide it, to use it. It's just information. Something, or someone, needs to act upon that information. It would be like imagining that a computer somehow just evolved. As impossible as that would be, the problem remains. A computer can't do anything on its own. It needs power and programs. Then, it needs a person to use all the information to produce a result. In the case of DNA, information alone is not life. It's in the energizing and use of the information, in very precise manners, that life comes into being. Evolution can neither produce the information, nor act upon it – *LIFE IS A GIFT FROM GOD!* ("In Him [Jesus] was <u>life</u>…" John 1:4;   "For in Him [Jesus] we live, and move, and have our being…" Acts 17:28;   Jesus said, "I am the way, the truth, and the <u>life</u>:" John 14:6.)

❋ Let's review what we've just covered in this lesson.

True or false:

1.   The story of the peppered moth is good evidence for evolution.   TRUE   FALSE

2.   The story of the peppered moth, if it were true, is actually just an example of natural selection at work.

     TRUE   FALSE

3.   A whale is a large fish.   TRUE   FALSE

4.   All fish are classed as mammals.   TRUE   FALSE

5.   Early insects ate only pollen.   TRUE   FALSE

6.   Some scientists believe that flowering plants were "invented" by dinosaurs. They have scientific

     evidence of this.   TRUE   FALSE

7.   "Eohippus" is the name of the first animal on the chart of horse evolution.   TRUE   FALSE

8.   "Eohippus" is actually a small horse.   TRUE   FALSE

9.   A vertebrate is an animal with a spinal column.   TRUE   FALSE

10. Flowers can think up ways to defend themselves.   TRUE   FALSE

11. A "vestigial organ" is supposedly a body part that no longer has usefulness.   TRUE   FALSE

12. There are many vestigial organs in all living creatures.   TRUE   FALSE

UNIT 5

"AUNT LUCY"

(Human Evolution)

MANKIND CAME FROM AN APE?

*P*eople who believe in evolution have tried for many years to prove somehow that their theory is correct. Surely, if mankind has been evolving for many years there would be some evidence of it. The most solid evidence of this would be found in two places.

1. It should be something we can observe happening.
2. There should be many, many fossils that indicate the changes from an ape to a man.

We've already covered the first one in an earlier lesson. What is OBSERVABLE and DEMONSTRABLE does <u>NOT</u> agree with evolution.

The second one is what we're going to look at now. Evolutionists claim that man has been evolving on Earth for 2 – 4 million years. If this is true, there should be millions upon millions of fossils showing all of these changes.

But, there aren't <u>ANY</u>!

Let's start by looking at some of the charts that are used to show what they believe. Ones like this first one on the right are often found in textbooks. They are designed to show, in picture form, the steps evolution has taken over time to form things from that first simple cell that they say developed on the earth 4½ billion years ago. That simple cell is on the bottom. As it divided and became many cells, over time all the
plants, insects, animals and birds formed. You can see that mankind is on the end of a branch that includes animals. In some textbooks, they put a caption under this chart that might say something like this:

"This chart shows how man evolved from a single-celled organism."

That is wrong! This chart shows nothing of the sort. To show "HOW" this happened would require many books explaining each tiny step of the way. It would need to show how mutations caused each of the millions of steps necessary between each kind of creature. Of course, as we have already seen, this is not science - because it's not observable. This chart is simply trying to show a LINK between the various kinds of creatures.

Scientists have hoped, for many years, to find what they call "links in the chain". For example, if some sort of fish turned into a frog, then there would have had to be a "fishfrog" at some time in the past. Or, if reptiles turned into birds, then surely "reptobirds" lived in the past. There should be millions upon millions of fossils of these creatures in the ground.

But, there aren't any! There are NONE!

That's why they're called "missing links". All of the fossils that are found are basically from the same kinds of creatures that we still have today. However, that hasn't stopped evolutionists from trying. They have dug up some bones over the years that have greatly excited their imaginations. Many of these bones have been used to try to show how man evolved from an ape-like creature. They have drawn charts that look like the one pictured here. Many people will look at a chart like

RAMAPITHECUS
AUSTRALOPITHECUS "Lucy"
HOMO HABILIS "1470 man"
HOMO ERECTUS "Peking / Java"
CRO-MAGNON
NEANDERTHAL
HOMO SAPIENS

this, and believe it simply because it looks reasonable. It shows the early ape on the far left, then on to other, slightly more human-like creatures, and on up to human beings (the last one on the chart). And, each HOMINID is given a name in Latin. A hominid is a creature supposedly evolving between the first ape and mankind. So, the six in the middle of this chart would be called hominids, or ape-men. Charts like this have been put in many textbooks and taught as though it is a fact.

But, many people who believe this chart don't know that most of the creatures that appear on it are made up from only bits and pieces of fossil bones. Many people think that the scientists have whole skeletons that show clearly that the chart is accurate. This is not true at all!

In the few lessons that will follow, you will see what kind of "evidence" has been used to make up these creatures — supposedly your ancestors!

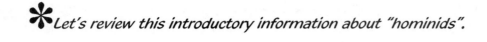 *Let's review this introductory information about "hominids".*

True or False:

1. According to evolution, mankind has been evolving on the earth for 2 – 4 million years.

    TRUE   FALSE

2. There should be millions of fossils that would serve as evidence for this.   TRUE   FALSE

3. Charts that have been developed to show evolution from the first, single-celled creature up to man show "how" these developments happened.   TRUE   FALSE

4. There are no fossils that show one kind of creature turning into another.   TRUE   FALSE

5. A "hominid" is the name given to a creature that is supposedly evolving between an "ape" and a man.

    TRUE   FALSE

APE-MEN: A CLOSER LOOK (Part 1)

We're going to briefly look at each of these creatures on the chart, starting from the first ape. Evolutionists say that mankind AND modern monkeys (including chimpanzees, baboons, etc.) all came from a common ancestor. They have drawn this as the first creature on the chart.

Already, there is a big problem. The first creature on the chart NEVER EXISTED. He was totally in the minds of certain evolutionists. He's completely made up. There aren't even any bones, or fragments of bones, to look at and discuss. Some evolutionists said that this creature was "believed" to have been a forest dweller, the ancestor from which both man and apes descend. But they admit that no traces of such a creature have yet been found.

Did you catch that? <u>No traces of such a creature have yet been found</u>. If there isn't even any evidence, why is this creature on the chart? That is not science AT ALL. This is pure guesswork. Even most evolutionists agree with that now. Most of them, including some famous ones, have admitted that it should not be on the chart.

What's next on the list? The first hominid. He's called Ramapithecus. The first such creature was completely made up from a piece of jawbone — two inches long!! Just imagine that. How can you tell, from a small piece of jawbone, how tall the creature was, how long its arms were, how much hair it had on its body, what its posture was, etc,? The point is — you can't! There have been some other little bones discovered over the years that have also been classed as Ramapithecus, but none of them are believed anymore to be your ancestors. That's right! Even the evolutionists have removed these creatures from the chart. They say that by 1981, Ramapithecus was dropped because evolutionists now believe that the bones they have of this creature are just from a fossilized ape, or a type of ape that perhaps is now extinct. There goes the second one off the chart.

Australopithecus is next. That name means "southern ape". That's a good name for it because that's exactly what it is — an ape. So, what bones have been discovered to indicate that these creatures were ancestors of yours? Again not much!

Some of the bones of these creatures were found among stones that some scientists think were tools. These were simple tools probably used to cut things up. So, the evolutionists say that this creature was the one who used the tools. But, how do they know that? Was anyone there to see them do it? Of course not. It is more reasonable to say that perhaps these small creatures were the ONES BEING CUT UP and eaten by humans who then moved on just as nomads do. You see, there's no way to know scientifically who used the tools. Evolutionists assume the monkey-like creature did. Creationists assume that humans did — and the ape-like creature was probably the victim. There are people in the world who still use stones like this today.

One of the most famous of these Australopithecines was named "Lucy" by Dr. Johanson, the man who discovered her. But, what was she — really?

Lucy is quite a small creature, and there's not very much of her. Dr. Johanson believes that Lucy walked upright just as humans do. He believes this because of the shape of Lucy's hip bones (many evolutionists disagree with this). Many of the other bones of her skeleton are missing. To the right is a picture of all the bones of Lucy in a museum.

Now, it is remarkable to note that even most evolutionists doubt that Lucy was an ancestor of human beings. They also say that she was most likely an extinct type of ape, being very similar to other "tree swingers"... apes and monkeys.

But, there are also some other interesting facts. First, her skeleton is only 40% complete! Some scientists say that it's actually less than that! That means that most of her isn't even there! How, then, can anyone say that they KNOW she's a hominid? That's actually just "wishful thinking".

Now, compare her skeleton to a regular, adult human skeleton (pictured on the left). She's only 3½ feet tall. Her small size should be a big hint as to her true identity. That's the size of a chimpanzee or a young gorilla — or an extinct species of one of them.

Also, most of her skull is missing, but most scientists say that, what there is of it is very similar to that of a gorilla.

So, even though there are still those who agree that Lucy was a hominid, most evolutionists disagree and have removed her from the list. Now, of the eight that were on the list to begin with, there are only five left. Are they hominids? Is there any scientific proof that they were our ancestors?

AUSTRALOPITHECUS
"Lucy"

✱ *Let's quickly review this part of the chart.*

True or False:

1. There is at least some evidence for the "early ape" from which both modern apes and man descended.

    TRUE   FALSE

2. Ramapithecus is no longer used by evolutionists; they say now that it was just an extinct ape.

    TRUE   FALSE

3. Australopithecus is the "southern ape".   TRUE   FALSE

4. The famous Australopithecine, "Tracy", was found by Dr. Johanson.   TRUE   FALSE

5. Most evolutionists agree that the "hominid" Dr. Johanson found was an ancestor of humans.

    TRUE   FALSE

6. Lucy's skeleton is very incomplete.

    TRUE   FALSE

7. It's very easy to tell what a creature looked like with just a few of its bones.

    TRUE   FALSE

85

APE-MEN: A CLOSER LOOK (Part 2)

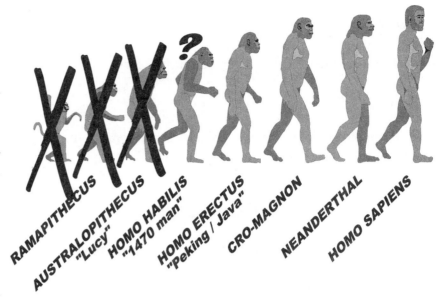

RAMAPITHECUS
AUSTRALOPITHECUS "Lucy"
HOMO HABILIS "1470 man"
HOMO ERECTUS "Peking / Java"
CRO-MAGNON
NEANDERTHAL
HOMO SAPIENS

We continue now with a look at Homo Habilis, the fourth one on the chart. One of the most famous of these is known as "1470 Man", or "Skull 1470" (so named because that is its number at the museum in Kenya, Africa, where the fossil is displayed). Only the skull was found, and this is a very interesting skull because of the age that evolutionists have given him. They have tried several ways to try to determine the age of this skull, and it turned out that every date they came up with makes the skull much older than they say it's supposed to be. Actually, one of the tests MADE THE SKULL OLDER THAN ALL THE ONES BEFORE HIM ON THE CHART! How can that be? He's in the middle! Something is wrong here, wouldn't you say? In fact, many evolutionists now claim that there was no such thing as Homo Habilis. Many believe that this creature was wrongly made up from various bones from other types of apes. That's why there is a question mark over him.

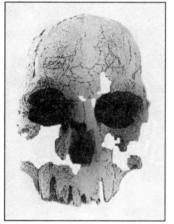

But, there is also a sad part to the story of this skull. You see, when evolution first became popular, part of what evolution taught is that certain black people were not as evolved as white people. Some groups of people were viewed as INFERIOR to others. This is racism, and the teachings of evolution were very supportive of racist ideas for many years. The Bible teaches that all human beings are part of Adam's family. We're ALL part of the human race. No race is INFERIOR (or not as highly evolved) as another. All humans are made in the very image of God!

When fragments of a skull like "1470 Man" (above) are found, nobody knows what the creature looked like. But evolutionists often hire artists to draw the creature the way they WANT it to have looked. So, using the skull pictured above, they have had artists draw pictures like this one at the right.

Ask yourself some questions. How would an artist know what the hair looked like? Did they know that he had a monkey-shaped nose?... or monkey lips?....or dark skin color? The point is, THEY CAN'T KNOW THOSE THINGS! It's only the theory of evolution that says what the creature looked like. This, again, is NOT science! This is the kind of bad "science" that should be completely avoided.

86

The racism part of evolution teachings produced a very sad story in the United States. Early in the 20ᵗʰ century, the Bronx Zoo put a black man from the African country of Togo in the zoo in a cage near the apes, monkeys and baboons. His name was Ota Benga. He was put there as an example of a person who was still evolving. Even though the zoo denied this, everyone knew that's the reason he was there. Curious people would gawk at him and kids would poke fun at him. Eventually, he was let out of his cage during daytime, but would go back in at night. Later on, Ota Benga committed suicide. He killed himself. He had become bitter and lonely. He had been convinced that he was not important; he was just a "curiosity" for people to stare at. How sad and tragic! He was a human being, made in God's image – just like you and me!

Ota Benga 1881-1916

The next one on the chart is Homo Erectus. Evolutionists believe that they have some very good examples of this creature, and over the years there have been a number of fossils found that support this idea. However, what do the fossils actually show? The two most famous of the Homo Erectus examples are "Peking Man" and "Java Man". Let's look at each of these.

Peking Man was discovered in China at what appeared to be an old mining site outside the modern city of Beijing. No skeletons were found – mainly just pieces of skulls. But, they seem to have disappeared. Some people believe that they were lost on a ship that sunk during World War II, so the original finds aren't around to examine any more. However, some of the dug-up specimens appear to be completely ape-like.

Other examples of Homo Erectus are found in various countries, and many scientists say that they can't see much of a difference between these specimens and human beings. There are some small variations, but those can be easily explained by differences in diet, climate, family history, etc. They all appear to be in the normal range of differences that we see in humans today. Also, fossilized bones of humans and Homo Erectus specimens have been found in rocks that supposedly are from the same time period – meaning that they lived at the same time, perhaps together!

Another Homo Erectus discovery, in Africa, is called Turkana Boy. Much of his skeleton is present, and he is listed among the Homo Erectus specimens, BUT most scientists consider him to be completely human! What does that tell you?! No ape-man here!

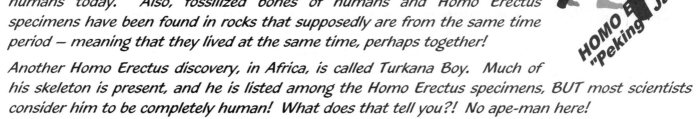

Another famous Homo Erectus hominid is Java Man. A skull cap was discovered by Eugene Dubois in 1891 on the island of Java in the South Pacific. One year later he found a leg bone 50 feet away. What do you do with a skull cap and a leg bone? You call it a hominid, of course. At least, that's what Eugene Dubois did – and many people believed him! Why did they believe him? Because he had definitely discovered an ancestor of humans? No, they believed him because they **WANTED TO BELIEVE** that he had found real evidence. Many evolutionists have tried to find evidence over the years for their theory, and some of them seem willing to believe almost anything to support their beliefs. Eugene Dubois knew all along that the skull cap he had found was from a creature like the one at the left – a gibbon (a large ape with no tail), and that the leg bone was from a human!

87

So, again it appears that there's just another link that's still missing. You see, a lot of this type of "evidence" is believed, not because it is a fact, but simply because it helps to support the theory of evolution. People choose what they want to believe in, and many people have already chosen to believe in evolution. Most of them, then, will choose to believe whatever "evidence" is brought forth, often in newspapers, magazines, TV programs, and in schools.

The next one on the list is Cro-Magnon Man. He was discovered in caves in France. Actually, quite a number of bones were found in these caves. But, more than that, paintings were discovered on the walls. These paintings are typical of many paintings on cave walls. Scenes of animals are common in caves. In fact, there are still some tribal people who do it today.

So, what was the evidence for Cro-Magnon Man? Human bones and paintings in caves! Does that sound like good evidence to you that these creatures were ape-men? Of course not, but it made a good "cave man" story, though. Here is the interesting part: Even the evolutionists agree now! They now admit that Cro-Magnon people were completely human. They say that they were just hunters living in caves. In fact, you can hardly even find any information on Cro-Magnon Man any more. Evolutionists have completely removed him as a hominid. He's completely human!

Who's next? Neanderthal Man. Who was he? Neanderthal Man was so named because of some bones that were found in the Neander Valley in Germany. Some of the skeletons were slightly bent over. There were also some skulls that had slightly different shapes than modern humans. These findings gave evolutionists the idea that these were ape-like creatures, not quite fully evolved. Neanderthal Man has become one of the most famous "hominids" on the earth. He appears in many textbooks and museums.

But, it appears that the evolutionists made another mistake. Scientists found that the reason that some of the skeletons were slightly bent was because these people suffered from diseases that made them that way. These diseases do the same things to people today! And, it turns out that the slightly different shape of some of the skulls is quite normal in some people who are alive today. This turns out to be the same story as Cro-Magnon Man. They're fully human.

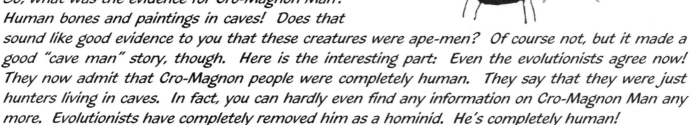

RAMAPITHECUS AUSTRALOPITHECUS "Lucy" HOMO HABILIS "1470 man" HOMO ERECTUS "Peking / Java" CRO-MAGNON NEANDERTHAL HOMO SAPIENS

Now, let's look at the chart. The one at the end is the only one we haven't discussed. He's you and me! - so he doesn't count. All the others are either apes, or fully human. So, where are all the missing links?

The missing links are still missing! They always will be because they don't exist!

NOTE: This has been a quick look at the basic chart, and it has covered just several examples of some of the major bones of various creatures that have been found over the years. Various fossils are discovered from time to time, and they usually wind up in one of the categories we've looked at, or a SUB-CATEGORY (some evolutionists think that there are several different creatures that belong in the same category). However, ALL fossils found wind up being human, or from apes or monkeys we still have today, or extinct ones. The purpose of this portion of the unit has simply been to show you *some* of what has been discovered and some of the methods used to interpret them.

NOTE: Remember, too that everyone is BIASED. What does that mean? It means that everyone looks at things from his or her own point of view. If a person is an evolutionist, then he will usually assume that any evidence found will support his view that living things evolved. If a person is a creationist, then he will usually assume that any evidence found will support his view that God created everything just as the Bible states. It is important to ask ourselves why we believe what we do. Remember that most people who say they believe in evolution believe it simply because it's the only thing they were ever taught. Many Christians are that way, too. Do you know what you believe? Do you know *why* you believe it? Is God's Word trustworthy?

*It's review time for this section.*

True or False:

1. The best known "Homo Habilis" skull is "1470 Man".   TRUE   FALSE

2. "1470 Man" is clearly an ape.   TRUE   FALSE

3. Evolutionists are able to know exactly what the "live" version of the fossilized bones looked like.

    TRUE   FALSE

4. Evolution's early teachings included much racist thought.   TRUE   FALSE

5. "Peking Man" and the skull cap of "Java Man" were both apes.   TRUE   FALSE

6. "Java Man" turned out to be the skull cap from a gibbon and a leg bone of a human.

    TRUE   FALSE

7. "Cro-Magnon Man" and "Neanderthal Man" are excellent examples of hominids.

    TRUE   FALSE

APE-MEN: A CLOSER LOOK (Part 3)

*F*inally, we'll look at other hominids that some evolutionists have made up to try to show that you and I evolved from an ape. (By the way, new fossils are being found all the time. Occasionally, some of these are classified as hominids, too, and given new names not shown in these lessons. However, they ALL, in the end, turn out to be either apes or man! – not "ape-men"!)

Perhaps one of the most famous of these is "Piltdown Man". In 1912, several bits of bone were discovered in a gravel pit in England. They were pieces of a skull and a jaw. The skull looked very much like a human skull, but the jaw was very much like an ape's jaw. So, this was exciting news for the evolutionists. At last, they had their evidence. Newspapers around the world carried this amazing story. Many famous scientists agreed that this was proof of evolution.

This fossil stood proudly on the side of evolution for about 40 years. Then, it all came crashing down! It turned out to be a fake! Someone had paired up a real human skull with the jaw from an orangutan. The bones were stained with a special chemical to make them look old. Also, the teeth were filed to make them look more authentic. All scientists know now that this was a fake.

This isn't the only example of bad science. There's also the story of "Nebraska Man". But, there wasn't a skeleton, or even several bones to show that he existed. In fact, all there was to Nebraska Man was ONE TOOTH! But, he became famous! Why?

At the time the tooth was discovered (1922), many fossil bones like this were being used as evidence for evolution (evolutionist scientists still do this today, of course). Back then, it was illegal to teach evolution in schools like it's taught today, so some evolutionists decided to challenge that law. A very public trial took place in Tennessee in 1925 called "The Scopes Monkey Trial". A mockery was made of creation, and evolution was presented as a theory worthy of being taught in the schools because of all the evidence. Guess what "evidence" was used in court by the evolutionists? The tooth! The Piltdown bones were also used as confirmation. Because of the publicity of this trial, the teaching of evolution was eventually permitted in the public school classrooms. Now, however, ONLY evolution is permitted – nothing else!

The saddest part of this story, though, is that two years after the trial, scientists went back to the site where the tooth was discovered in Nebraska. They found the other remaining parts of the creature.....it was a type of pig! So, partly because of a pig's tooth (and a fake skull) evolution is now taught in public schools. THAT is what makes Nebraska Man famous. Of course, this discovery was embarrassing, but it accomplished their goal. Faulty evidence was used at a trial. Faulty science was used to get evolution into schools, and it keeps it there today. Should this be tolerated?

Is this science? I wonder how many people died during those 40 years who were fooled into believing a lie. How many other lies are going on in the name of science that try to prove false ideas like evolution? We need to pay close attention to the Bible. It warns us about following any false ideas.

> ...avoiding profane and vain babblings, and oppositions of knowledge falsely so called.
> I Tim. 6:20 (KJV)

You might think that all of the hoaxes happened long ago. Surely that kind of thing doesn't happen now any more, right?

Think again!

As recently as 1972, there was another ape-man story that made its way around the world. This time, the story came out of the Philippines. There, on one of the islands, a tribe of "evolving creatures" was found! They were known as the "Tasaday". It wasn't long before photographers and journalists were sent to the island to bring the story back to their homelands. The only easy way in was by helicopter. Soon, the helicopters bringing newsmen started arriving in the jungle to see the ape-men for themselves.

They had a wonderful time among these naked "ape-men". They photographed them climbing trees, sitting in their  caves, and using their "stone-age" tools. The people in the rest of the world who were seeing these pictures and reading the stories were amazed to see a tribe of people that time seemed to have forgotten.

It was going very well (for those who chose to believe this) until it was discovered to be a big hoax! Someone from the government was trying to get attention and fame. He knew just what to do. If he could provide the world with a bit of evidence for evolution that it wanted so desperately, then he could get the publicity he wanted. So, he came up with this plan and told the Tasaday people exactly how to act, look and sound to seem like ape-men.

Well, it worked for a while and perhaps fooled many people. Why? Maybe it's because they WANTED it to be evidence for evolution. Or, perhaps people often just believe what they read! People who refuse to believe the Bible will continue to willingly allow themselves to be fooled by many different ideas like this. The Bible makes it clear that we were created in God's image. We are not animals. Humans are not related to animals. We are unique.

Now, as we finish this unit, there is one other very interesting point to consider.....

We've been told that we evolved from ape-like creatures over a period of about 3-4 million years. If that's true, think about all of your ancestors that would have lived! Starting millions of years ago from just two creatures that would have produced all of the humans and apes in the world today, there would have had to be an ENORMOUS number of hominids that have lived over that time period. We're not talking about millions of them, or even billions of them — there would have been MANY times that! Where are their bones?!

Think about it. All these creatures would have been mostly just hunter-gatherers. That means that they would have lived off the land, finding whatever they could to eat - monkeys don't farm!

Therefore, they would have mostly had to live in the warm areas of the world where food would be available all year long. This area is known as the TROPICAL ZONE. Look at the world map to the left. The area between the black lines is the tropical zone. Most of the earth's land is OUTSIDE the tropical zone, which means that these creatures could not have lived there year round. That area gets too cold in winter, and very little food can grow there at that time. Therefore, most of these creatures would have had to live in a pretty small area of the world, and these warmer areas of the world should be absolutely choked with billions of bones from your "ancestors". Almost anywhere you would dig for this evidence — especially in valleys where they would have most likely lived — you should find them easily. Again, where are they?!

They're not there! They never were!

However, it's only been about 4,000–5,000 years since the great flood, and only eight people survived it. They started the population growing again afterwards, so if you figure on a reasonable population growth rate since that time, you could easily arrive at the number of people living on the earth today!

Which proposal do you think is more reasonable?

Hey! What about this idea instead?......

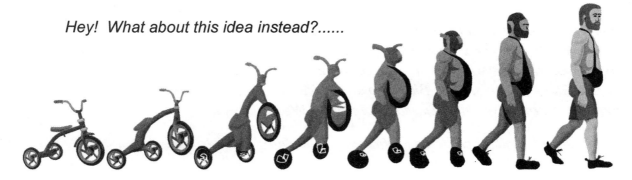

92

UNIT 6

MAN IS WITHOUT EXCUSE

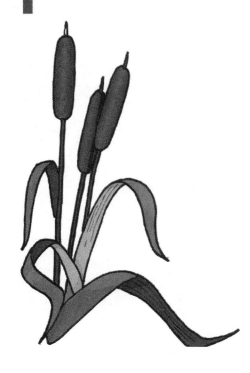

ROMANS 1:20

*A*n interesting truth about creation is found in the New Testament book written by the apostle Paul to the people in Rome. It's found in the first chapter of that book, in the 20th verse.

✱ *Read Romans 1:20, then answer the following questions:*

1. What can be clearly seen? _____

2. What are God's invisible qualities? a. _____

   b. _____

3. How can these qualities be clearly seen? _____

   _____

4. *THINK!* Why are people without excuse? _____

   _____

The verse that we've just looked at is fascinating because it shows us that even though we cannot prove that God exists by science, and we cannot prove by science that God created, it shows us that the EVIDENCE for His existence and creation are overwhelming. Evidence gives you a reason to believe something. Evidence tends to prove something you believe in. This verse says that God's very nature is shown in the things He made. Living things contain so much evidence they had a designer that God says mankind is without excuse. Human beings will never be able to stand before

their Creator after they die and say, "I never knew there was a God!!" God will say to these people that the evidence for His existence and handiwork was all around – if they had bothered to look! As we have already seen in a previous lesson, living things are far too complex to even consider the idea that they came about by natural chance. This verse is saying, "Look around you! The evidence that there is a God is everywhere!"

With that in mind, the next few lessons will help us to understand this. We will look at a few living creatures, some of the things they can do and why they do them. We will look at instinct, animal disguises, animal weapons, and why creatures are the size that they are compared to you and me.

THOSE AMAZING ANIMALS! (A quick look)

*E*very animal alive is a miracle. Each creature, no matter how we humans might despise it (such as a fly or a mosquito), is an incredible work of genius. Each creature has been specially designed and they can accomplish amazing tasks.

Just watch some common creatures sometime. How does a spider know where and how to spin her web so perfectly? How does a fly land upside-down on the ceiling? How does a lightning bug make real light? How does a new butterfly know where to find food, especially since it has eaten *ONLY LEAVES* up to this point? How can fruit flies find fruit that is wrapped up in layers of plastic? How do robins find worms? How does a Venus flytrap work?

Every creature is complete with all it needs to be able to survive its normal life span and REPRODUCE (make more of its own kind). If evolution was true, we should still be seeing all kinds of creatures struggling and dying with half-evolved parts that don't work right yet. Of course, you probably couldn't see this anyway because such creatures would be very soon extinct.

So, let's forget the story of evolution now, and go on a "safari" to look at a few amazing animals from around the world.

AUSTRALIA

Let's start off in Australia. Many years ago explorers discovered large mounds on the ground. At first they thought that the mounds were graves of the native people who lived in the area. They soon discovered that the mounds were built by birds, called Mallee fowl. These birds have an amazing ability that could never be explained by the accidents of evolution.

They dig a hole three feet deep in the ground. Then they put leaves and other vegetation in the hole, and cover it back up with sand and dirt to form a mound. The vegetation begins to rot and so keeps the ground warm. The female Mallee fowl then lays her eggs in the mound. The male keeps guard over them to make sure the temperature stays exactly what it is supposed to, and he changes the shape of the mound to do this. When the

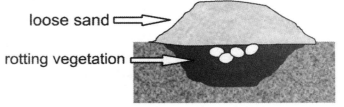

loose sand ⇦

rotting vegetation ⇦

temperature gets too hot from the decaying leaves deep in the mound, he uncovers them to let some air circulate around them. When the sun begins to get hot, he covers them deeply again to protect them. This sounds amazing. But it's even more amazing how he does this.

The eggs must stay at 91½°F. If the temperature goes up by one degree, the baby chick dies. If it goes down by one degree, the baby chick dies! How does the male know what the temperature should be? How does he keep the temperature so perfect? He has a built-in thermometer in his beak! (I suppose that thermometer got there by accident?) And, that's not all! When the chicks hatch, they are about three feet underground. They have about 15 hours of hard work in front of them digging their way out. How do they know what to do and which direction to go? If you hatched any other kind of bird under the ground like this, it would simply die!

When you think of all the things the male, the female, and the chicks must automatically know in order to survive, it becomes very easy to see that these abilities did certainly not come about by evolution. This shows amazing design!

AFRICA

Let's go over to Africa next, and have a look at a giraffe. Giraffes have BIG problems....or at least, they should have. They are so big, and they have such a unique shape, that they should have all kinds of problems with their blood vessels (veins and arteries that carry blood). But, God has taken care of the giraffe's special needs. Let's look at one.

When a giraffe wants to drink, it has a problem. Its head is 16 - 18 feet up in the air, so it's not easy for it to drink. First, it has to make sure there are no predators, like lions, in the area. Then it approaches the water. Next, it has to spread its front legs out to lower the front half of its body. But that's not enough. Now, it has to bend its front legs to lower the body even more. Then, it can lower its head to the water to drink – just like this one is doing in the picture to the right.

But, that would cause another big problem for the giraffe. All the blood in the huge neck would go racing way down to the head, causing severe problems or even death for the giraffe. At very least, when it puts its head back up after drinking, it would pass out and fall over when all that blood would go rushing back out of its head. But none of those problems happens. Why?

God has placed special valves in the giraffes' necks so that when they put their heads down, the blood flow stops and doesn't rush down to the brain. A little bit actually does get there, but God provided a special "sponge" at the base of the brain that absorbs the blood that gets there so that the giraffe has no problems.

Ask yourself......how did these things get there? Do you think the giraffe grew these body parts by accident, or were they designed that way from the beginning?

Also from Africa comes the strange story of the honeyguide and the honey badger – a fascinating look at a SYMBIOTIC RELATIONSHIP (what in the world does THAT mean?). That big term is simply used to describe some different kinds of animals that directly need each other to stay alive.

The honeyguide is a little bird that eats bee grubs (baby bees), honey and wax. The problem is that when a honeyguide discovers a beehive, it can't get into the hive to eat these things because the bees would sting it to death. So, the little bird flies off to find a honey badger. This is a mammal that looks a bit like a big skunk.

The badger will then follow the special calls that the honeyguide is making, and the bird will lead the badger to the beehive. The badger is specially made to rip open the hive and get at the honey, which it needs to survive. When he's done, the little honeyguide gets to eat all of the "leftovers" – which he really enjoys!

Ask yourself.....how did the honeyguide (a bird) and the honey badger (a mammal) get this strange relationship? Of all the birds that chirp every day, why does the badger only follow the honeyguide's call? Who told the honeyguide to look for a badger to help it get its meal?

96

Let's stay in Africa for one more — the chameleon. This is one of the strangest creatures in the world. One of the reasons for this is the chameleon's incredible ability to change color to match its surroundings. In its natural environment, it can become automatically camouflaged on almost anything it walks on or in, and it doesn't even know it is happening. Look at this photograph. Can you see the chameleon? You can quickly get an idea of how well the chameleon in the picture blends in with his surroundings. And, he is sitting out in the open! They *really* disappear in the shade!

Many people in Africa kill chameleons out of fear of them because they can see how almost "magically" the chameleon can change its color, so these people think that there is a demon living inside the creature! Of course that's not true! But then, how did it get this amazing ability? By evolutionary chance? Certainly not! Only God could have made something like this!

NORTH AMERICA

For our last stop on this short safari, let's visit a special kind of beetle that can do something that baffles the people who study it. It's found in many places, including North America - the bombardier beetle. Some evolutionists try to explain how the parts of this unique beetle came into being by random chance, but they only fool themselves.

What's so special about this beetle? He has a "cannon" at the back end of his body to defend himself! What does he shoot from this cannon? A very smelly liquid that's also very, very hot! In fact, it's so hot that it's at the boiling point of water! But that's not all. He can also aim his cannon in different directions depending on where his enemy is. Figures A and B show him doing this.

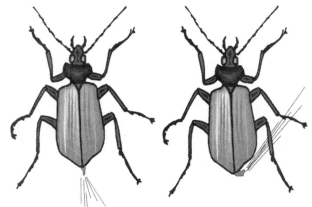

Figure A   Figure B

In order for the beetle to be able to do this, he had to have been designed. There is absolutely no other reasonable explanation for it.

There are thousands upon thousands of creatures that could be looked at in a lesson such as this. We have only briefly looked at five. Perhaps you can find many more to study!

THOSE AMAZING ANIMALS! (Instinct)

If you've spent any time watching natural animal behavior, you've probably asked this simple question at some time: "How do they know how to do that?!" For example, in the spring of the year, we all see birds returning to our yards to build nests. Many of us see lots of robins busy at work. But, ask yourself these questions:

1. Who told the robin that she has to build a nest?
2. Who told her where to build it?
3. Who told her what materials to use to build it?
4. Who told her how big it should be?
5. Who told her what shape it should be?
6. Who told her that her eggs have to go inside the nest?
7. Who told her to sit on the eggs, and for how long?
8. Who told her to feed the chicks when they hatch?
9. Who told her what to feed them, and how often?
10. Who told her when her job is done?

Did the robin go to the "Robin School of Nest Building and Baby Care"? *No, she has never learned these things from any other living creature. She knows these things by* INSTINCT. *Instinct is a free education that God has built into each creature. Instinct cannot be learned. It's automatically passed down from parent animals to their babies. Instinct helps creatures to survive as long as they stay in their natural environment.*

Many creatures can learn certain things. For example, you can teach a dog to do tricks. You can train circus animals in the same way. But, this is not instinct. If you train an animal, only that animal can do the trick you trained it to do. But actions that an animal does by instinct are also done by <u>all</u> *of the same kind of animal. All robins know, by instinct, how to build a nest. But if you caught a robin, tamed it, then taught it to do tricks, then only your robin can do what you specifically taught it to do.*

Let's look at this a little closer. If you became hungry, what would you do? Perhaps you would think to yourself, "Boy! I'm hungry. I think I'll go to the kitchen, where I know there is food, and find some bread and some other things in the refrigerator to make a sandwich." You would think this because you have a brain that can reason things through. You might also think about something to drink or some snacks to go

along with your sandwich. And, you might decide that you're not in the mood for milk – you'd rather have a soda today. Your brain can reason and choose, and then you have your meal. But, many creatures cannot think this way.

98

For example, consider a flower for a minute. Flowers are usually brightly colored. Why? For one thing, God made them that way because they're beautiful to look at. But He also did that for another reason. The flowers are like flags waving to the bees and butterflies. Those insects know, by instinct, to go to the flowers. By instinct they also know what to do when they get there. Nobody taught them this. It's automatic!

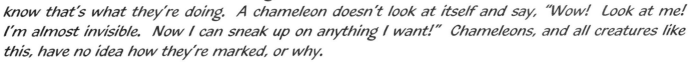

But, look closely at this drawing of a flower. Right in the middle there's a spider – waiting! What is she waiting for? You and I know that she's waiting for a meal, BUT THE SPIDER DOES NOT KNOW THAT.

Many creatures, like the chameleon we looked at in a previous lesson, are camouflaged. God has done this so that creatures can hide from each other, even though those creatures don't know that's what they're doing. A chameleon doesn't look at itself and say, "Wow! Look at me! I'm almost invisible. Now I can sneak up on anything I want!" Chameleons, and all creatures like this, have no idea how they're marked, or why.

Let's go back to the spider on the flower. Many spiders don't spin webs to catch creatures. Some jump on their prey. Others, like the crab spider, wait for an insect to just walk into their "arms". That's what's going on in this drawing. The crab spider is camouflaged to look like the flower. She walks to the middle of the flower where the nectar is (the food that the insects are after), and waits there with her legs open wide. BUT, she has no idea why! She does not know WHAT nectar is, or WHERE it is. She does not know what a butterfly is. She does not know what ANY other creature is. She does not know what the flower is. She does not know that any insects are coming to the flower. She does not even know why she is there! She cannot think like you and I can. She is purely acting on instinct. If she obeys her instinct, eventually an insect will walk right up to her without even knowing she's there. Then, again by instinct, she will slowly start spinning a thread around the insect until it can't get away.

Virtually all creatures in nature act this way. They don't think about what they're doing, or why. They just do it, obeying what God told them to do by instinct. This will help their SPECIES (the specific kind of creature that they are) to survive. Animals are like robots, programmed (like a computer) by God to act and respond in certain ways in their own environment.

Look at this moth. The drawing on the left shows her relaxed. But, if something startles her, like a bird coming up to eat her, she lifts up her two upper wings. Why does she do that? SHE HAS NO IDEA WHY! She just does it by instinct. But, you and I can see that the wings underneath now make the whole moth look like a creature with big eyes and even a nose. That might scare the attacker away. But the moth has never even seen the fake eyes on her wings. Even if she had, she would have no idea what they are or what they look like.

What creatures can you find around your house that act in this way?

THOSE AMAZING ANIMALS! (Size)

If everything is just an accident, like evolution teaches, how is it that everything in nature is the perfect size compared to everything else? For example, why are you the size you are compared to trees? Why do most trees grow much bigger than you and I? Imagine if the tallest trees in the world were tiny - just 12 inches tall? Can you imagine how terrible that would be? We would have no shade in the summertime. Fruit would be incredibly tiny. We wouldn't have any wood to build things with. We probably would also die from lack of oxygen! Why do trees grow to the perfect size to help us. Is that an accident of nature?

Let's take our imagination even farther. Imagine if you woke up one day and saw a pile of earth outside in your front yard. You go out to look at it and notice that there's a hole right in the middle. You walk up to the pile and peer down

into the hole. Suddenly, a huge ant, the size of <u>you</u>, comes running up out of that hole! First of all, if it wants to eat you, could you run faster than it? I don't think so! Second, if it caught you, would you be able to overpower it? NO!

Ants are incredibly strong for their size. They're designed that way. God has a special job for them to do all over the world. In most places, where you find life, you also find ants. They are nature's perfect little garbage collectors. Wherever they are found, they're found in great numbers. Our whole nature system wouldn't work if ants were huge. They're perfect just the size they are!

Now, let's make this idea more interesting...... Have you ever been stung by a bee? Most of us have. What about a mosquito, or a yellow jacket? Again, most of us know what it's like to be stung by one of these. It's not a pleasant experience. It itches, or it hurts! This causes us to fear that creature the next time we see one coming around.

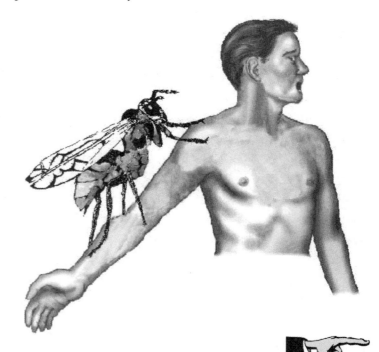

The question is: Why aren't these creatures much bigger? Why isn't a mosquito as big as a crow? Why aren't bees as big as robins? Why isn't a wasp as big as your arm? If they were and stung you, you probably wouldn't survive. Your body probably couldn't handle that amount of poison.

But, that's not all!

There are many, tiny insects that have very dangerous poisons. But, these bugs are so small that the poison really doesn't hurt us. In many cases, you hardly even feel it, or there might be a slight itch. If you think about it, we've all been stung by many creatures. If they were much larger, we would all be dead. So....why are they the size they are compared to you and me? An accident?

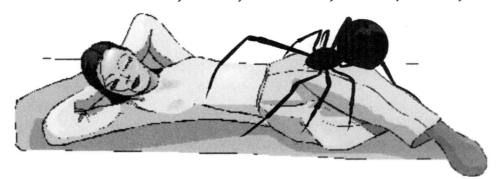

Imagine if you were asleep, and you woke up because something was walking on you. You turn on the light and discover that it's a giant spider! What would you do?! Well, you'd probably realize after a few moments of panic, that it was just a bad dream! But, again, why aren't spiders that big? Most spiders are very small – some are so tiny that you need a powerful magnifying glass to see them. Is this just another accident? And what is it that spiders actually do? They keep the insect population down. Spiders are everywhere. They lurk all through bushes, grass, and shrubs catching and eating many of the bugs that hatch out. If spiders weren't there in great abundance, you and I could never go outside on a nice, warm day. The bugs would immediately be in your hair, your face, in your mouth.....! We can be thankful not only that they are the size they are, but also that they are abundant.

Finally, let's look at just one more creature that is small in the real world, but would make a drastic difference if they were much larger – caterpillars! Caterpillars eat huge quantities of leaves.

Imagine if all caterpillars were the size of the one in this picture. Well, if they were, you and I would be dead. Why? Because they would eat us? No, but imagine what they would eat! They would kill off all the trees in the world, and then life for the rest of living creatures, especially humans, could not continue.

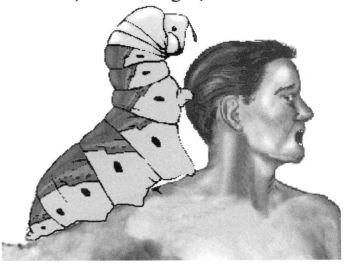

Now, imagine the next step in the life of this caterpillar. Soon, it will be a butterfly. If the caterpillars were this size, how big will the butterflies be? They'll be huge! How long will they live? They won't live long at all because they won't find anything to eat. When their wings finally fill out and they can fly, they'll head off instinctively looking for a flower. When they land on the flower, they will be way too huge for it. They will try to get the nectar out using the special tube they have, and it will be way too big!

The flowers (including the ones on fruit trees and on vegetable plants), that desperately need the bees and the butterflies to pollinate them, are perfectly matched in size to those insects. If they weren't, everything would soon die!

Amazing accident? Or amazing design? -- If God so carefully designed all the animals for specific jobs, how much more must He have a plan (a job) for <u>us</u> to do?!

#6 Unit Test

UNIT 7

DINOSAURS

DINOSAURS: WHAT WERE THEY?

Many people are fascinated by dinosaurs these days. When we walk into a natural history museum, there are often huge fossil dinosaur skeletons on display. In fact, many people go to these museums just to see these skeletons. People have lots of questions about these creatures that once roamed many places on the earth. What were they? When did they live? What happened to them? Why do we find fossils of many kinds of dinosaurs in the ground? Why were they so big? Are there any dinosaurs today? Does the Bible talk about dinosaurs?

Textbooks, museums, and movies are full of "answers" to many of these questions. Unfortunately, most of them use evolutionary ideas, so their answers reflect only that view. The topic of dinosaurs is very popular, and many evolutionists have used it very effectively to get their views widely known. Most people now, when they hear the word "dinosaur", think only in terms of "millions of years".

In the next few lessons, we will look at the answers to these questions from the Bible's point of view. Even though the Bible does not use the word "dinosaur", it does provide us with the answers to some of these questions.

Let's start with the word itself – dinosaur. This word was unknown before 1840. Not long before that, people had begun to discover strange fossils that couldn't be identified. They were sure they had found teeth – but from what? The more these and other bones were discovered, the more scientists figured that these were from creatures unknown to man. A scientist by the name of Sir Richard Owen, who had studied the fossils of several of these new creatures, believed that a whole new type of animal had been discovered. Everyone was sure that these animals were reptiles, and if that was the case, scientists could only imagine what they must have looked like. These would certainly have been terrible lizards, so that is the name Sir Richard Owen gave them in 1841. Scientists give Latin names to creatures that they study, so in Latin, "terrible lizard" is "deino sauros" – or dinosaur.

Iguanodon ("iguana tooth") – the first dinosaur discovered.

The rest is history! From that time on, there has been a mad dash to discover new dinosaurs. And, people have been very successful at this. Many new types, or SPECIES, have been discovered since those early years, and they have fascinated people all over the world since then.

So, what were they? Dinosaurs are considered by all scientists (evolutionists and creationists) to be land-dwelling reptiles. They had many of the CHARACTERISTICS *(or body features) that modern reptiles have, but there are differences.*

Let's first consider some of the characteristics of reptiles:

1. Most reptiles hatch out of eggs. Modern reptile eggs are not like bird eggs, which are brittle-shelled. Reptile eggs feel more like leather. Most scientists agree that dinosaurs also hatched out of eggs. Many fossils of reptile eggs have been discovered, and many of them are believed to be from dinosaurs. Some of these eggs appear cracked, so there is also the possibility that dinosaur eggs were more brittle than modern reptile eggs. The largest fossilized eggs that have ever been discovered are about 18 inches long.

2. Another characteristic of reptiles is that they have scales on their skin, and this is believed to be true of most dinosaurs, too. A scale is part of the reptile's skin. Evolutionists believe that somehow a form of reptile turned into a bird. A common belief is that the scales turned into feathers. Of course, this is not true. As we have seen in an earlier lesson, one kind of creature cannot turn into another kind. Also, there are <u>no fossils</u> that show that reptiles turned into birds. There have been interesting fossils discovered in China that many evolutionists use as "proof" that this happened, but they do not show any such thing! (In fact, some have been shown to be fakes!)

The legs of modern reptiles grow from the sides of their bodies. Dinosaur legs grew so that the weight of their bodies was above their legs.

3. A big difference between modern reptiles and dinosaurs is the position of their legs. The legs of modern lizards, including crocodiles and alligators, grow out to the sides of their bodies. They basically crawl on their bellies. However, most creatures that we would call dinosaurs walked more like a mammal – with their legs beneath their bodies, not to the side.

4. Reptiles are cold-blooded. That means that they must get their warmth from the sun, or some other source. When a mammal, which is warm-blooded, eats food, most of that food is used to keep the animal at a certain temperature all the time. In humans, that temperature is 98.6°. Scientists are assuming that dinosaurs were also cold-blooded. That is a reasonable thing to believe since modern reptiles are cold-blooded.

5. One of the more interesting things about many reptiles is that they never stop growing as long as they are alive. After hatching out of its egg, a reptile grows to MATURITY - it becomes an adult. Once it becomes an adult, its rate of growth slows way down, but some types keep growing until they die. This is an interesting point because it might explain why some of the dinosaurs grew so large. Most dinosaur eggs are about the size of crocodile eggs, or smaller. Crocodiles grow to about 16 feet long when they reach maturity. They live up to 70 years (sometimes longer), and since they don't stop growing, an old crocodile can be a monster of more than 20 feet! That's a terrible lizard! But, think about it: Could we perhaps learn anything about dinosaurs from this?

How big were dinosaurs, and what were were they like?

There are many things we can learn about dinosaurs from the fossils we find. For example, we can see clearly how big many of them were. Some grew to enormous lengths. Some dinosaurs, like T. rex, have caused many people's imaginations to run wild. All it takes is a look at the skull of this creature! It looks fierce. It has long, sharp teeth. It's very large.

Clearly, the T. rex was a fierce, meat-eating dinosaur, right? Not necessarily. It _might_ have been, but since nobody who is alive today has ever seen a live T. rex, it's impossible to know that. His long, sharp teeth prove only that he had long, sharp teeth!

Movies have been made that feature these creatures (and others, too) as mean, bloodthirsty hunters who shake the ground when they walk. They will smash vehicles and anything else to get at humans. They are rampaging, untamable beasts that destroy anything in their path.

Is that the truth? Is that the way reptiles act today? No, they don't. Remember that there is no way to know how a creature acted just by looking at its teeth, or any of the rest of the skeleton.

Now, what about their size? How big were dinosaurs? Many people think that dinosaurs were huge creatures. Actually, only a few were large. The average size of dinosaurs was the size of a large dog. Some were as small as little chickens! But, how many people want to go to a museum and look at little chicken-sized dinosaurs? No, they want to go and see the huge ones. But, the large ones are actually quite rare. Take T. rex, for example. Only about a dozen have ever been found!

Why were some of these creatures so large? Well, obviously God designed them that way. But, some are so large that they've been given names like "Ultrasaur" and "Gigantosaurus". There might be a special reason that some huge types got that big. Do you remember how long people could live before the flood? They could live over 900 years. If people could live that long, could the animals have lived that long, too? Perhaps they could have. Now, if a dinosaur never stopped growing as long as it was alive (since it's a reptile), _it could well be that the very large dinosaurs were just very old dinosaurs!_ For example, imagine that God designed a Diplodocus to be 80 ft. long when it's grown up. But, if that Diplodocus could live for 900 years, it might grow to 100 ft. in length, and be given a name like "Ultrasaur" when its bones are found.

We must be careful to point out that this is just a possibility. There are some scientists who disagree with this idea, and they might be right, but it's an interesting thought.

✱ *Let's review what we're learned about dinosaurs.*

True or False:

1. Evolutionists have given us very good answers to the questions about dinosaurs.

    TRUE   FALSE

2. Before the year 1840, the word "dinosaur" was used only when referring to large creatures.

    TRUE   FALSE

3. The word "dinosaur" means "terrible lizard".   TRUE   FALSE

4. The name "iguanodon" means "iguana tooth".   TRUE   FALSE

5. Dinosaurs are believed to be land-dwelling reptiles.   TRUE   FALSE

6. Most reptiles lay eggs.   TRUE   FALSE

7. There are several fossils that clearly show a reptile turning into a bird.   TRUE   FALSE

8. There are no differences between modern reptiles and dinosaurs.   TRUE   FALSE

9. Most scientists believe that dinosaurs were warm-blooded.   TRUE   FALSE

10. Most reptiles never stop growing as long as they are alive.   TRUE   FALSE

11. The very large dinosaurs might have been old ones.   TRUE   FALSE

12. Dinosaurs have always been portrayed accurately in movies.   TRUE   FALSE

DINOSAURS: TWO DIFFERENT VIEWS

At this point, it will be useful to review what the evolutionists teach about dinosaurs. This will show how different man's ideas are compared to God's.

The evolutionists' dinosaur story....

Evolutionists say that the earth is billions of years old. That time is divided into five basic periods. You can see them here on the geological column. The first two periods took over 4 billion years. This is when the "simple" life was forming in the sea.

The third period is called the PALAEOZOIC PERIOD, *which simply means "ancient life" and covers the next 325 million years. The next major period of time is called the* MESOZOIC PERIOD, *which means "middle life". This period lasted about 180 million years. The last period is called the* CENOZOIC PERIOD, *meaning "recent life", and it has lasted up to now — about 65 million years.*

Evolutionists teach that the dinosaurs lived during the Mesozoic Period. But, they also teach that the dinosaurs didn't all live at the same time. They say that as some dinosaurs went extinct after millions of years, other new types evolved to take their place. During the whole 180 million years of this period, many dinosaurs "ruled the earth", but at different times.

Finally, at the end of this period, about 65 million years ago, something terrible happened on the earth that caused all, or at least most, of the dinosaurs that were alive to go extinct. They claim that a big ASTEROID *(a giant ball of rock in space) might have struck the earth and caused such terrible conditions on the earth that these creatures couldn't survive.*

Naturally, if dinosaurs went extinct 65 million years ago, no man has ever seen one since we humans have only been evolving for the last 2 – 4 million years.

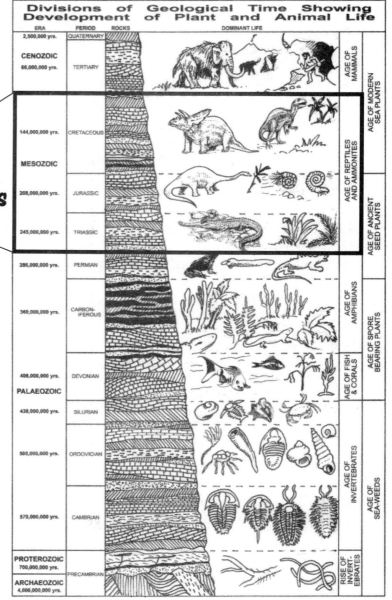

The Bible's version....

The Bible tells a very different story about how dinosaurs came to be on the earth, when they lived, and what happened to them. To tell it, we are first going to draw a timeline from creation to now.

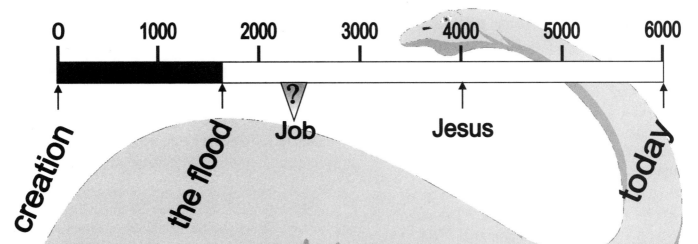

0   1000   2000   3000   4000   5000   6000

creation   the flood   Job   Jesus   today

Before we continue, let's understand what the timeline means, and where it comes from. In the Bible, there are several listings, or genealogies, of the line of men from Adam to Jesus. We can add up the years that are there and see that from the creation to today is about 6,000 years. The numbers at the top of the line show this. Every 1,000-year period is numbered.

Below the line you can see when events happened that are important to the Bible's account of dinosaurs. You can also see when two people lived – Job and Jesus.

Now, let's add the dates to those people and events. First, creation took place right at the beginning. The flood started 1,656 years after creation. Job was born several hundred years after the flood ended, but we really don't know when (we'll see later why Job is important). Jesus lived roughly 4,000 years after creation, and about 2,000 years earlier than we are living today.

With these things in mind, let's look at the questions about dinosaurs. First, when did they live? Well, ask yourself this question: When did God make them? Genesis 1:24 – 25 make it clear that God made all the creatures that live on land on day #6 of the creation. That would include reptiles. That would also include the dinosaurs. But, God made something else on day #6, too – or rather, He made SOMEONE. God made Adam and Eve. That means that MANKIND AND DINOSAURS HAVE ALWAYS LIVED TOGETHER! They don't have 60 million years between them like evolution teaches. They were made on the same day!

Dinosaurs lived with man for 1,656 years. By the way, there was never an age when dinosaurs "ruled the earth", as evolutionists claim. God gave that job to mankind.

At the end of the 1,656 years, there was a terrible catastrophe that wiped out the dinosaurs, though not completely. And, it wasn't an asteroid hitting the earth, as evolutionists suppose. It was a terrible flood that came during the lifetime of Noah. Now, look at the timeline. The black area is the time that the dinosaurs lived on the earth.

The dinosaurs weren't completely wiped out, though. We know from the Bible that Noah built an ark, a floating box, to protect two of each kind of animal and to keep their kind alive on the earth once the flood was over. This terrible, world-wide flood not only destroyed the dinosaurs, but also all living things that live on dry ground and breathe air through their nostrils (Genesis 7:22).

Of course, this brings up another question: Were dinosaurs on the ark? The answer is YES. How do we know this? We know this specifically by Genesis 6:19-22. In these verses we learn this:

1. God told Noah to take with him 2 of every kind of animal onto the ark. The question is: Is a dinosaur a "kind" of animal? Yes. (vs. 19)
2. God himself brought the animals to Noah to put into the ark. Noah didn't have to go out looking for them. Did God forget any animals? No, He brought them all. (vs. 20)
3. Noah obeyed God. (vs. 22)
4. Furthermore, we know that dinosaurs were still alive at the time the flood started because we find their fossilized bones in the strata layers *put down by the flood.*

So, since God told Noah to take 2 of each kind of animal onto the ark, and since God was the one who brought the animals to Noah, and since the Bible says that Noah obeyed God, we can be sure that dinosaurs were on the ark.

Sometimes, this brings up another question: How could a huge brachiosaur fit on the ark? The answer is: Brachiosaurs (and all creatures) don't start off huge, do they? 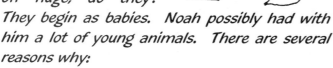 They begin as babies. Noah possibly had with him a lot of young animals. There are several reasons why:

1. Young animals might be healthier than adults.
2. Young animals don't take up much room.
3. Young animals don't eat as much as adults.
4. They don't produce as much waste as adults.
5. Young animals sleep a lot.
6. Young animals don't fight with each other.

〰〰〰〰〰〰〰〰〰〰〰〰〰〰〰〰〰〰〰

We've seen when dinosaurs were made. We know now when they lived. And, we know what killed them (and all creatures that weren't on the ark). But, if they were on the ark, there's another question that needs to be asked: What happened to them when they came off the ark?

The simple answer to this question is.....we don't really know! But, there might be some answers based on things that we do know.

1. The world was very different after the flood. Perhaps the atmosphere was somewhat different, too. It might be that some of these animals couldn't survive under these new conditions or they might not have found enough to eat.
2. We don't know how fast dinosaurs were. It could be that many of them were caught by the other predators coming off the ark. After all, what were the tigers, leopards, cheetahs, etc. going to eat? Remember, all the other animals had died in the flood. The only other animals to eat were the ones coming off the ark!
3. It could be that as man increased in numbers, they themselves might have hunted dinosaurs to extinction. History books, including the Bible, speak of great hunters on the earth.
4. Or, perhaps the dinosaurs were a type of creature that was neither truly cold-blooded nor warm-blooded. Maybe they were totally different in that way from creatures alive today. Maybe something about them was totally unique to them. That might explain why all the dinosaurs, large and small, went extinct, while we still have lizards, large and small, today!
5. Remember that it's not only dinosaurs that have gone extinct since the flood. There are many other creatures that are now extinct, too. The question why dinosaurs went extinct has fascinated us basically because of the huge size to which some of them grew.

But, have dinosaurs actually gone extinct? Does the Bible talk about them at all? We'll see in the next lesson.

✱ *Let's review what we're learned about the two different views of dinosaurs.*

True or False:

1. The chart, called the "geological column", shows how evolutionists divide up time on the earth.

    TRUE   FALSE

2. Evolutionists say that dinosaurs lived during the Palaeozoic Period.   TRUE   FALSE

3. According to evolutionists, not all kinds of dinosaurs lived at the same time.   TRUE   FALSE

4. Evolutionists think that the age when dinosaurs lived came to an end about 95 million years ago.

    TRUE   FALSE

5. According to evolution theory, no man has ever seen a true dinosaur.   TRUE   FALSE

6. The Bible tells us when God made the dinosaurs.   TRUE   FALSE

7. The word "dinosaur" is not found in the Bible.   TRUE   FALSE

8. Mankind was ruled by the dinosaurs for a long time.   TRUE   FALSE

9. The flood of Noah's time is the disaster that nearly wiped out the dinosaurs.   TRUE   FALSE

10. The flood didn't completely kill off the dinosaurs; some survived on the ark.   TRUE   FALSE

11. Unfortunately, animals like brachiosaurs were too big to fit on the ark.   TRUE   FALSE

12. Many animals have gone extinct since the flood – it's not just the dinosaurs.   TRUE   FALSE

DINOSAURS AFTER THE FLOOD

Are there any dinosaurs alive today?

*E*volutionists have told us for many years that dinosaurs are extinct. But, some of them are changing their minds about this. These people are saying that dinosaurs didn't go extinct after all — some of them turned into birds! They say this because they see some "similarities" between certain dinosaur bones and those of birds. So, they now teach that the birds you see in your yard are just very highly evolved dinosaurs! WOW! That takes quite a stretch of your imagination, wouldn't you say?

Dinosaurs might not all be extinct, though (but NOT because they turned into birds). There have been many creatures sighted at various times around the earth that might be dinosaurs, or at least, creatures associated with dinosaurs. There are reports of creatures that look just like pterodactyls. There are paintings on cave walls (obviously painted by people) that look like dinosaurs. There have been some reports of strange sea creatures that, according to evolutionists, lived only many millions of years ago. From central Africa come reports of very large creatures that look like brachiosaurs. They're called Mokele Mbembe (meaning "when it lies down, it dams up the streams").

Are these stories true? We don't know. The only way to know for sure is if one of these creatures could be caught. But, what would the evolutionists say if a creature like this was actually discovered — still alive today? Would they give up evolution? Would they stop believing in it? Probably not, because something like this has already happened. Here's the story:

Fossils of a strange fish, called a coelacanth, were discovered long ago, and evolutionists have believed that this fish has been extinct for at least 65 million years. But, they say that it is a VERY important discovery. Why? Because evolutionists believe that this fish is a link between fish and amphibians, like frogs. They say that the fins look like they were evolving into legs.

Again, this was just a hopeful guess. The fins don't look like that at all. They're just a special type of fin! But it doesn't matter anyway, because in 1938 a LIVE coelacanth was caught off the east coast of Africa. IT LOOKED <u>EXACTLY</u> THE SAME AS THE FOSSIL! How can that be?! They were supposed to have turned into frogs long ago!

This was another surprise for evolutionists. But, it didn't change their mind about evolution. They simply called the coelacanth a "living fossil". What does that mean? It is the name evolutionists give to any fossilized creature that's supposed to be extinct long ago, but is discovered to be still living. They simply say that, for some "mysterious" reason, evolution didn't touch that creature over the millions upon millions of years.

Isn't it strange that evolution wouldn't change a fish one bit over many millions of years, but then they tell us that you and I evolved from an ape-like creature in just 2-4 million years? So, even if we found all kinds of dinosaurs alive today, most evolutionists would probably just call them "living fossils" and continue believing as they always have.

Does the Bible say anything about these creatures?

*T*here are many references to "dragons" in the Bible. Usually, these were understood to be great beasts either living in the water, or monsters living on land. Perhaps these were dinosaurs that were still alive at the time the books were written.

But, there are two places in the Bible where the creatures described are clearly very large reptiles. These descriptions fit dinosaurs almost perfectly. Both of these creatures are found in the Old Testament book of Job. The first one is described in Job 40, and the second in Job 41. So, we know that some dinosaurs survived for at least several hundred years after the flood.

In these two passages, God is talking to Job and describing some of His creation. He first talks about BEHEMOTH, in Job 40. Then He talks about LEVIATHAN. God tells Job to go and look at these creatures. He wouldn't tell Job to do this if they weren't still alive for Job to see. (By the way, these two words might not sound like dinosaur names to you. That's because they are Hebrew words. The Old Testament was written in Hebrew.)

✳ Read Job 40:15–24 and all of Job 41.

BEHEMOTH – Many people think that this creature is an elephant, or a hippo or rhino. In fact, the footnotes in many Bibles even say this. (Remember that footnotes are NOT part of the inspired Word of God. They are simply put there by the publisher to help understand difficult passages.) In this case, they are wrong.

First, elephants mainly eat from trees. Behemoth eats grass (vs. 15). Second, the cedar trees in Job's time were huge trees that would sway in the wind. That's why God says that behemoth sways his tail like a cedar. An elephant has a tiny little tail. So do hippos and rhinos. They are not at all like the one described in Job 40. What God was describing to Job was a creature like this one – perhaps a brachiosaur or a Diplodocus.

Does an elephant's tail look like this?

It's the same thing in Job 41. Many people think that leviathan is a crocodile. They say that the "fire" that comes from his mouth must be his tongue sticking out like a snake does. This is wrong. Crocodiles do not, and CANNOT, move their tongues like that.

Another reason we know that leviathan is not a crocodile is that you cannot pierce leviathan's skin with a spear, a sword, or dart (vs. 26). But, you can use any one of those weapons to kill a crocodile.

Many Christians feel embarrassed by leviathan. They think that he's just a myth from old folklore, and they can't understand why he's included in the Bible if "fire-breathing dragons" are just a myth. The problem here is not with the Bible. The problem is with their thinking. Just because we don't see "fire-breathing dragons" today, does that mean that they didn't exist at some time in the past?

Let's just imagine that fireflies, or lightning bugs, suddenly went extinct for some reason. Now, let's imagine that 2,000 years pass by, and someone opens up an old history book and reads that there were lightning bugs in our day. They might laugh and say, "What!! Two thousand years ago there were little beetles that flew around at night with lights on their rear ends?! Oh, come on!! That's just nonsense!" Would they be right? No, of course not. Just because

they don't see the lightning bugs doesn't mean that they didn't exist. We see them all the time in the early summer.

And, how about the bombardier beetles that we looked at in an earlier lesson? What if the same thing happened to them? What if they became extinct today and someone read about them 2,000 years from now? They might say the same thing some people say about fire-breathing dragons: "Oh, come on! You don't really believe that 2,000 years ago there were little beetles with cannons that could fire steam at 212°, do you?!"

The leviathan had the ability to make fire come out of its mouth, and smoke out of its nostrils just as the beetles have the ability to make light, and fire a cannon. How could leviathan do this? Perhaps by chemical reactions, or maybe by igniting gas. When a cow eats grass, it produces methane gas in its stomach. Methane gas is VERY flammable. Perhaps a leviathan had the ability to ignite gas coming up from his stomach.

Those stories you've perhaps read about knights of long ago going out and fighting dragons are probably based on true events of the past while these creatures were still alive. If you do a serious study of the "dragon legends" from England, Europe, Japan and China, you will find that those creatures are almost identical to the leviathan of Job 41!

The important thing to remember is this: If the Bible says that something is true, or that something happened, then it's TRUE and it DID HAPPEN!

114

✱*Dinosaurs after the flood? The subject is very interesting, and there are many stories about this. How many are true? We don't know. Undoubtedly, many are just fantasy. Wouldn't it be interesting to see a live one? Job did. Let's review what we studied in this lesson.*

True or False:

1. Some evolutionists are teaching us today that dinosaurs might not all have gone extinct. They say that some of them turned into birds!   TRUE   FALSE

2. If a dinosaur was actually found alive today, most evolutionists would immediately admit that evolution is wrong.   TRUE   FALSE

3. The coelacanth is a perfect example of what evolutionists call a "living fossil".   TRUE   FALSE

4. A "living fossil" is a fossil that's still alive.   TRUE   FALSE

5. Job chapters 40 & 41, in the Bible, give us examples of "living fossils".   TRUE   FALSE

6. A behemoth was a long-tailed elephant.   TRUE   FALSE

7. A leviathan is an example of fantasy in the Bible.   TRUE   FALSE

8. If the Bible says that something is true, then it's true!   TRUE   FALSE

Notice...

On the next sheet is a handout that you might find useful to give to people who have questions about dinosaurs. Remove the page, photocopy both sides (like it is here), then fold them down the middle.

#3 Unit Test

DINOSAURS!

Some Answers to
Some Common Questions

HOW "EVOLUTIONIZED" ARE YOU? TRY THIS QUIZ.

1. *Which of the following is the best example of a prehistoric animal?*
   - a. Crocodile
   - b. Woolly mammoth
   - c. Brachiosaur
   - d. All of the above
   - e. None of the above

2. *The "Age of Dinosaurs" and the "Age of Mammals" are separated by many millions of years.*
   - a. True
   - b. False
   - c. We can't know for sure
   - d. Only science has the answer

3. *Tyrannosaurus rex had long, sharp teeth. This creature was obviously always a meat-eater.*
   - a. True
   - b. False
   - c. We can't know for sure

4. *The "age when dinosaurs ruled" ended about 60 million years ago when an asteroid hit the earth.*
   - a. True
   - b. False

5. *Dinosaurs died out long before man emerged on Earth.*
   - a. True
   - b. False

Answers

1. e. None of the above. There is no such thing as a "prehistoric" animal. God gave us His account of history starting right at the beginning of history.

2. b. False. ALL land animals were made on the sixth day of the creation, so they all lived together, right from the beginning.

3. b. False. ALL animals and birds were originally designed as plant-eaters. Tyrannosaurus rex's long, sharp teeth prove only that he had long, sharp teeth!

4. b. False. Dinosaurs never "ruled" the earth. Mankind was given that responsibility. Also, the main period when they lived lasted about 1700 years and it ended at the time of the great flood of Noah's time - about 4,500 years ago.

5. b. False. Land-dwelling dinosaurs were created on the same day as man and coexisted on the earth with man until the flood. Some survived for a time afterwards.

Dinosaurs – some answers to the common questions

1. **What were dinosaurs?**
Basically, dinosaurs were types of land-dwelling reptiles. The name "dinosaur" means "terrible lizard" because some were very large. Dinosaurs had a special skeletal structure.

2. **How big were they?**
Many were very small. Others, like diplodocus were up to 100 feet long. Ultrasaurus weighed as much as 200,000 pounds. The average size was like a big dog or small horse.

3. **When did they live?**
Basically, they lived from the time of creation up to the flood of Noah's time. Some survived for a while afterwards.

4. **When were dinosaurs created?**
The land-dwelling dinosaurs were created on the sixth day of the creation. Marine and airborne creatures were created on day five.

5. **How did they get their names?**
Dinosaur names are always Greek or Latin. These are very old languages, and scientists have always named organisms they are working on in these languages so that scientists all over the world can understand the names.

6. **What are fossils?**
Fossils are the traces or impressions in rock of past living organisms.

7. **Why do we find fossils of dinosaurs today?**
We find billions of fossils of all kids of creatures and plants that lived in the past, not just dinosaurs. Fossils are only made under very precise conditions, which the great flood would have produced. Dinosaur fossils are simply some of the most impressive because of the size to which some grew.

8. **Did all creatures associated with dinosaurs look like big lizards?**
No. Some (like the plesiosaur) lived in the sea, while others (like the pteranadon) flew.

9. **Were there any dinosaurs on Noah's ark?**
Certainly. Like most other creatures, Noah took two of each kind of dinosaur onto the ark.

10. **If so, how could they fit?**
Probably most creatures were young, so they were smaller. Even so, the ark was very large. It measured 450 ft. long, 75 ft. wide, and 45 ft. high, and it had three decks.

11. **Why did they go extinct?**
With the exception of those on the ark, all creatures that lived on land and breathed air through nostrils, including the dinosaurs, died during the flood. When people and animals came off the ark, the world was very different. Probably there were no more lush forests (at least initially) that might have provided food for a large dinosaur. Also, the predators (like lions) possibly brought a lot of animals to extinction right away because there were only two of most types. The large carnivores possibly died out because their food source was also dying out. Man also might have caused many extinctions through hunting. Atmospheric conditions, or perhaps a unique metabolism, might have hurt these reptiles.

12. **Why were some dinosaurs so large?**
Some reptiles are larger than others by design, just like a crocodile is larger than a chameleon. Dinosaurs were reptiles, too. Most reptiles never stop growing throughout their life. Before the flood, people lived much longer than they do today - over 900 years. Scientists are not sure why this was so, but perhaps animals could live a long time, too. If this was true of dinosaurs, and if they never stopped growing while they were alive, possibly the very large dinosaurs were just old dinosaurs.

13. **Are dinosaurs mentioned in the Bible?**
Yes, at least one type of dinosaur is mentioned. In Job 40, God refers to "behemoth" and gives a description so detailed that it can be nothing but a "dinosaur. A strange, water reptile ("leviathan") is described in Job 41.

14. **Are there any dinosaurs alive today?**
The term "dinosaur" refers to certain types of reptiles that are extinct, but there are several very large lizards alive today. Crocodiles, alligators and Komodo dragons are good examples. However, supposedly extinct creatures (associated with the "dinosaur era") have been reported in several places around the world, on land and in the sea.

CONCLUSION

We have just looked at the creation vs. evolution issue in a basic way. There is much, much more information on this topic that can be studied. There are some excellent resources available that take each of these topics and greatly expand them. There are many good books and videos that can help in this way. We hope you have enjoyed learning about this issue, and certainly, that you now have a better understanding of the Bible's view on this subject. Hopefully, your faith in the accuracy of the Bible has been strengthened.

Now that the main part of this course is finished, we want to have one more opportunity to put into practice what we've learned. There are many people in the world who scoff at the Genesis account of origins and they claim that it's either not accurate, or just a fantasy – folklore. Unfortunately, some of these people claim to believe the rest of the Bible just the way it's written. This makes them very dangerous. They cause much confusion to people who are trying to make sense out of the world, why things are the way they are, and what the Bible has to say. People like this create doubt in the minds of others that the Bible is trustworthy.

On the next pages is a bit of a "final exam". There is no answer sheet. This is just an exercise to see how easily you can spot error. Stories very similar to the one you are about to read can actually be found on the Internet and in various books and videos. The story sounds so reasonable, but it is a death trap to faith in God's Word. You will see that there is enough "God" and "creation" included in the story to make it sound like a reasonable account of the true creation. BUT.......watch out!

God's Word has stood the test of time. It has come to us through much rich history, and protected by God Himself so we know what He wants us to know. God's Word stands, no matter how much people have tried, over the years, to change it to suit themselves.

Evolution is one of the seriously anti-Christian and anti-Bible teachings of the times in which we live. We make a very serious mistake when we try to mix it with the Bible.

Let's figure it out...

The following is a made-up story of how the earth and life came about. But, it is very similar to what some people actually teach. These people rewrite the creation account according to their beliefs that evolutionary sequences and dating are true, even though they may claim not to believe in evolution itself. So, they make up stories like this that sound good, but they certainly aren't what the Bible teaches. Can you spot the errors?

✱ *Read this story. Then, using a highlighter pen, highlight the parts of this story that you know are different from the true story of creation.*

In the beginning there were no plants, no oceans, no mountains, no sun, no moon, no stars…nothing. Only God existed. Then, He created space, time, matter and energy. Out of this sudden beginning, called the "Big Bang", all the stars and galaxies formed. Much later, the planets formed. At that time, billions of years ago, the earth could not have supported any kind of life. It had to cool down.

Then God's spirit moved over the surface of the ocean. This is when God first created life – in the sea. This was simple, single-celled life. Later, God allowed the clouds to start letting light from the sun through. God then caused water to start evaporating so that it could start raining on the earth. Then God gathered the water together in one place and dry land appeared. These became the oceans and the continents.

God changed the clouds again so that the overcast skies would occasionally break up to allow sunlight, moonlight and starlight through. He also created the atmosphere so that the animals He was about to create would be protected from harmful rays from the sun.

Then God made complicated creatures both in the oceans and on land. The first creatures He made were tiny worms. Then, as millions of years passed, He created other small animals. Some had shells on the outside of their bodies, like spiders, insects and crabs. Fish came next, then frogs, then reptiles.

God then created dinosaurs. They ruled the earth for about 100 million years, but a disaster took place about 65 million years ago that wiped out the dinosaurs. Some scientists think a huge asteroid hit the earth. The dinosaurs were not the only creatures to be destroyed by this. Many others were, too. All living things go extinct eventually even if there aren't big disasters. Advanced animals, like elephants and tigers, can go extinct in just a few million years. But simple animals, like beetles, may last over 150 million years. This is why God, during the time He was creating on the earth, had to constantly replace these extinct creatures with new ones.

After the dinosaurs, God created birds and mammals. Then, about 4 million years ago God began creating man-like mammals called "hominids". These creatures eventually learned to stand up on their two hind feet and began to use simple wood and stone tools. Some hominids painted scenes on the walls of caves. Others learned to bury their own dead. But, they were very different from us in several ways. They had no spirit or conscience like we humans do. They could not worship God. After several million years, these man-like creatures became extinct. Then, about 6 – 10 thousand years ago, God replaced them with Adam and Eve. From these two have come all the human beings that live on the earth today.

> ### Does this sound like the Bible's account of creation?

On this page, write down why this story is wrong in the places you highlighted. Write down what the Bible actually says. What parts are just made up?

_____

_____

_____

_____

_____

_____

_____

_____

_____

_____

_____

_____

_____

_____

_____

_____

_____

_____

_____

_____

_____

_____

_____

_____

_____

_____

#7

Unit One - The Creation

1 - Why Study Genesis? – no worksheet

2 - The Creation

1. 6 days
2. He gathered it to one place.
3. Day # 3.
4. Day #5.
5. Day #6.
6. Day #6.
7. It was good; very good.
8. The earth.
9. Sun, moon, stars
10. Man – seed-bearing plant, and every tree with fruit with seed in it.
    Animals – every green plant.

3 - Day #6

1. From the dust of the ground.
2. Streams came up from the earth
3. In the Garden of Eden.
4. The tree of life; the tree of the knowledge of good and evil.
5. Tigris, Euphrates, Pishon, Gihon.
6. To take care of the Garden of Eden.
7. The tree of the knowledge of good and evil.
8. No.
9. Livestock, birds, and beasts of the field.
10. A suitable helper.
11. A rib from Adam.
12. She was taken from man.

4 - How Long was a Creation Day? – no worksheet

5 - Origins

1. Origin of the earth.
2. Origin of dry ground.
3. Origin of vegetation and trees.
4. Origin of sea creatures and birds.
5. Origin of man.
6. Everything was perfect at the beginning.
7. Origin of man working.
8. Origin of the need for a man to marry.
9. Origin of woman.
10. Origin of marriage.

Unit Two – The Fall of Man & The Beginning of Nations

6 - The Fall of Man

1. B
2. C
3. A
4. C
5. C
6. D
7. A
8. B

7 - Sin's Penalty & Payment

1. All people; the glory of God.
2. Death; eternal life; Jesus Christ.
3. God; While we were yet sinners, Christ died for us.
4. Anyone; "Jesus is Lord"; God raised Jesus from the dead; you will be saved.
5. No; by grace through faith; your own works that cannot save you.
6. Perish.

8 - The Patriarchs (Part 1)

1. murder – verse 8.
2. offerings to God – verses 3-4.
3. building a city – verse 17.
4. nomads – verse 20.
5. flute & harp – verse 21.
6. forging of bronze & iron – verse 22.
7. men calling on the name of the Lord – verse 26.

9 - The Patriarchs (Part 2) – name search game

10 - The Patriarchs (Part 3)

You should have finished at the "game reserve".

Unit Three – The Flood

11 - God's Plan: Destruction!

1. Man's great wickedness; the earth was corrupt & full of violence.
2. The destruction of men, animals & birds.
3. The earth.
4. Noah.
5. He was righteous among the people of his time.
6. Build an ark.
7. Pitch.

8. 450 ft.; 75 ft.; 45 ft.
9. He wasn't. God was going to bring them.
10. Noah was to take all the food on board the ark.

12 - The Ark

1. kind
2. 522
3. three
4. breath
5. 120
6. FALSE
7. FALSE
8. TRUE
9. TRUE

13 - The Flood!

1. God told him that He would send the flood in seven days.
2. 600 years old.
3. eight.
4. In the six hundredth year of Noah's life, on the seventeenth day of the second month.
5. The waters that the earth had been founded upon, or formed from.
6. Forty days and nights.
7. Because these creatures do not breathe air through nostrils.
8. ALL the HIGH MOUNTAINS under the ENTIRE HEAVENS were COVERED.
9. 150 days.

14 - The Flood Recedes

1. FALSE
2. TRUE
3. TRUE
4. FALSE
5. TRUE
6. TRUE
7. TRUE
8. FALSE
9. TRUE
10. TRUE

15 - A New Beginning

1. Be fruitful and increase in number and fill the earth.
2. No.
3. Meat.
4. Meat with blood still in it.
5. He is made in the image of God.
6. By man shall his blood be shed.
7. Never again will the waters destroy the earth and life.
8. A rainbow.

16 - The Phases of the Earth – no worksheet

17 - Flood Evidence Today – no worksheet

18 - Fossils

1. That by God's Word the heavens existed and the earth was formed out of water and by water.
2. Water.
3. By God's Word.
4. By the waters that the earth was founded upon.
5. They are being reserved for a judgment by fire.
6. Because mankind is ungodly.
7. God will; by the power of His own word.

19 - The Nations

1. Nimrod.
2. One language.
3. Shinar.
4. A city with a tower that reaches to the heavens.
5. Baked bricks.
6. To make a name for themselves, and to not be scattered over the earth.
7. He confused their language; He scattered them over all the earth.

Unit Four – Science versus Evolution

20 - A look at Science – no worksheet (experiment)

21 - The Pillars of Evolution

1. knowledge.
2. a. demonstrable.
   b. repeatable.
   c. observable.
3. faith.
4. fact; theory.
5. a. "big bang".
   b. "non-living to living".
   c. "simple to complex".
6. time.

22 - The Big Bang

1. whole galaxies.
2. more order.
3. sun.
4. spin.
5. TRUE
6. FALSE

7. FALSE
8. TRUE
9. FALSE
10. FALSE

Essay – refer to text.

23 - Chemicals Come to Life?

Highlighted Words:
Believe; believe; might have; think; no set has been agreed upon; could have; believe; may have; might have; possibly; theories sparked the imagination; theory.

24 - Simple Life Becomes Complex? (Part 1)

1. TRUE
2. TRUE
3. TRUE
4. FALSE
5. TRUE
6. FALSE
7. TRUE
8. TRUE
9. a. ingest nutrients.
   b. store & use energy, and get rid of wastes.
   c. reproduce.
   d. grow and move.
10. the fittest survive.

25 - Simple Life Becomes Complex? (Part 2)

1. DNA
2. mutation
3. more complex
4. observed
5. kind

26 - How Old is the Earth?

1. FALSE
2. TRUE
3. FALSE
4. FALSE
5. FALSE
6. TRUE
7. TRUE
8. FALSE
9. TRUE
10. FALSE

27 - Evolution: Odds & Ends

1. FALSE
2. TRUE
3. FALSE
4. FALSE
5. FALSE
6. FALSE
7. TRUE
8. FALSE
9. TRUE
10. FALSE
11. TRUE
12. FALSE

Unit Five – "Aunt Lucy"

28 - Mankind Came from an Ape?

1. TRUE
2. TRUE
3. FALSE
4. TRUE
5. TRUE

29 - Ape-Men: A Closer Look (Part 1)

1. FALSE
2. TRUE
3. TRUE
4. FALSE ("Lucy")
5. FALSE
6. TRUE

Essay – refer to text.

30 - Ape-Men: A Closer Look (Part 2)

1. TRUE
2. FALSE
3. FALSE
4. TRUE
5. TRUE
6. TRUE
7. FALSE

31 - Ape-Men: A Closer Look (Part 3) – no worksheet.

Unit Six – Man is Without Excuse

32 - Romans 1:20

1. God's invisible qualities.
2. a. His eternal power
   b. His divine nature
3. They can be understood through what has been made.
4. Nature provides us with clear evidence that God is real.

33 - Those Amazing Animals (A quick look) – no worksheet.

34 - Those Amazing Animals (Instinct) – no worksheet.

35 - Those Amazing Animals (Size) – no worksheet.

Unit Seven – Dinosaurs

36 - Dinosaurs: What Were They?

1. FALSE
2. FALSE
3. TRUE
4. TRUE
5. TRUE
6. TRUE
7. FALSE
8. FALSE
9. FALSE
10. TRUE
11. TRUE
12. FALSE

37 - Dinosaurs: Two Different Views

1. TRUE
2. FALSE
3. TRUE
4. FALSE
5. TRUE
6. TRUE
7. TRUE
8. FALSE
9. TRUE
10. TRUE
11. FALSE
12. TRUE

38 - Dinosaurs after the Flood

1. TRUE
2. FALSE
3. TRUE
4. FALSE
5. FALSE
6. FALSE
7. FALSE
8. TRUE

Unit One

1. C	3. A	5. D	7. A	9. B
2. A	4. C	6. D	8. B	

10. Bible
11. a. To understand the world, past and present, or
    b. To recognize and refute compromise, or
    c. To help build Godly values back into society.
12. Reason or purpose.
13. Lie.
14. Adam – day 6   Trees – day 3   Moon – day 4
    Fish – day 5   Light – day 1   Birds – day 5
15. Sea, oceans, or water.
16. Dust of the earth.
17. Tigris, Euphrates, Pishon, or Gihon.
18. Tree of the Knowledge of Good and Evil.
19. Origin of Species.
20. Time.

Unit Two

1. A	3. B	5. E	7. C	9. B
2. B	4. E	6. B	8. A	10. D

11. Cain
12. Seth
13. Methuselah. 969.
14. Jubal
15. bronze. iron.
16. Enoch
17. good, or perfect
18. simple, or primitive
19. better, or more complex
20. Noah

Unit Three

1. C	4. D	7. C	10. A	13. D
2. B	5. B	8. D	11. A	14. A
3. A	6. A	9. A	12. B	

15. meat
16. rainbow
17. strata (sedimentary layers), little or no erosion between strata layers, marine fossils on all the mountain ranges of the world, or polystrate fossils.
18. Shinar

19. He confused the language.
    He spread people over the whole earth.
20. Any four of these: 1. the creation, 2. the fall of man, 3. the flood, 4. the events at Babel, 5. the cross.

Unit Four

1. C	4. B	7. A	10. C
2. E	5. A	8. B	11. B
3. E	6. A	9. B	12. B

13. a. observable
    b. demonstrable
    c. repeatable
14. living things
15. DNA
16. old

Unit Five

1. B	3. A	5. E	7. D
2. D	4. A	6. A	8. B

Unit Six

1. A	3. B	5. B	7. D	9. C
2. C	4. B	6. D	8. A	10. B

11. eternal power, divine nature
12. excuse
13. Australia
14. small
15. evidence

Unit Seven

1. D	3. A	5. C	7. A	9. D
2. E	4. A	6. A	8. B	10. A

11. scales
12. cold-blooded
13. 18
14. dog
15. "middle life"
16. 6,000
17. flood
18. God
19. behemoth
20. leviathan

UNIT ONE - TEST

Circle the letter of the correct answer for each of the following questions:

1. Evolution teaches that…

    A - All things came into being by chance, then God allowed things to become more complex.
    B - God created everything, then by chance everything became more complex.
    C - All things came to being by chance, then, also by chance, became more complex.
    D - God made things over billions of years.

2. If evolution is true, then…

    A - There is no such thing as RIGHT or WRONG.
    B - There is a purpose, a reason, for your existence.
    C - It won't make any difference in society if people believe it.
    D - We have hope when we die.

3. The creation versus evolution issue is really a spiritual issue.

    A - True   B - False

4. Genesis chapter 2 is…

    A - A different version of creation.
    B - A description of events that took place after the six days of creation.
    C - A more detailed description of the events of the sixth day of creation.
    D - A chapter that was added to the Bible by mistake.

5. To create everything in the universe, it took God…

    A - 7 days.   B – millions of years.   C - we don't really know.   D - 6 literal days.

6. Where was the Garden of Eden located?

    A - In present-day Middle-East.
    B - In present-day Europe.
    C - In present-day South America.
    D - We can't know.

7. The whole CREATION MODEL is best understood by studying…

    A - Genesis chapters 1 – 11.
    B - Genesis chapter 1.
    C - Evolution.
    D - Genesis chapters 1 – 51.

8. It doesn't make any difference if a creation day was a day, or a million years.

    A - True   B - False

9. It is OK to interpret the Bible by studying what the scientists say about it.

    A - True   B - False

Write the correct answer in the space provided:

10. The _____ is the source of the information on creation.

11. Give two reasons why we should study the book of Genesis.

    a._____

    b._____

12. If you were created, there is a special _____ for your existence.

13. The teachings of evolution have replaced the truth with a _____.

14. Next to each created item, write the number of the day on which it was created.

    Adam _____   Trees _____   Moon _____

    Fish _____   Light _____   Birds _____

15. According to evolution, life began in the _____.

16. God formed Adam from the _____.

17. Give the names of two of the headwaters at Eden.

    a. _____

    b. _____

18. From what tree was Adam not allowed to eat? _____

19. Charles Darwin wrote a famous book entitled: _____

20. If evolution was to be believable, then huge amounts of _____ were needed for it to have taken place.

UNIT TWO - TEST

Circle the letter of the correct answer for each of the following questions:

1. The Bible teaches that, in the beginning, Adam…

    A - was made "perfect", and in the image of God.
    B - was made as a sinful being.
    C - was deceived by the serpent.
    D - did not know God.

2. The Garden of Eden…

    A - was just a fictional place.
    B - was a real place, where Adam sinned against God.
    C - was where Cain killed Abel.
    D - was where Adam and Eve lived for the rest of their lives..

3. God made the first clothing Adam and Eve ever wore.

    A - True   B - False

4. God's curse included that …

    A - man was alienated (separated) from God.
    B - man would now have to work hard for his food.
    C - women would have great pains in childbirth.
    D - the serpent would have to crawl on its belly.
    E - all of the above.
    F - none of the above.

5. Sin is…

    A - man's basic problem.
    B - "missing the mark" of God's perfection.
    C - one of the central themes of the Bible.
    D - paid for only by Jesus' death on the cross.
    E - all of the above.
    F - none of the above.

6. Who has sinned?

    A - Only Eve.   B - All mankind.   C - Only the serpent.   D - Only Adam.

7. What is the penalty for sin?

    A - Mankind will now have to do good works to get to heaven.
    B - Temporary separation from God while mankind is alive on the earth.
    C - Death, physical and spiritual.
    D - There is no real penalty for sin.

8. Only Jesus has paid for sin and can forgive it.

    A - True   B - False

133

9. It really doesn't make any difference if the events of Genesis are true or not.

    A - True   B - False

10. A patriarch ...

    A - is a person who has never sinned.
    B - was found only in the Garden of Eden.
    C - is someone who invents something.
    D - a father or leader of a family or tribe.

Write the correct answer in the space provided:

11. The first murder in history was committed by _____.

12. Abel was replaced by _____ .

13. _____ was the oldest man who ever lived, and he lived _____ years.

14. _____ became the "father" of all who play the harp and flute.

15. Tubal-Cain produced all kinds of tools made from _____ and _____.

16. _____ walked with God; then he was no more, because God took him away."

17. According to the "creation model", at the very beginning, man was made_____.

18. According to the "evolution model" everything was _____ at the beginning.

19. According to the "evolution model", things have gotten _____ over time.

20. _____ was considered by God to be righteous among the people of his time. He had three sons who survived a disaster with him.

134

UNIT THREE - TEST

Circle the letter of the correct answer for each of the following questions:

1. In Genesis chapter 6, we read that God is grieved. Why?

    A - Because people have not spread out over the earth as He commanded.
    B - Because animals have become carnivores.
    C - Because mankind is wicked, and their hearts are bent on evil only.
    D - Because mankind kept eating the forbidden fruit.

2. God told Noah to cover the ark with pitch only on the outside.

    A - TRUE   B - FALSE

3. Who brought the animals to Noah's ark?

    A - God   B - Noah   C - Noah's sons   D - Other people

4. The only creatures taken on board the ark were…

    A - the "clean" animals.
    B - the kinds made on day six of the creation.
    C - birds and mammals.
    D - land-based creatures that have the breath of life in their nostrils.

5. A "species" of animal is the same as a "kind".

    A - TRUE   B - FALSE

6. The ark looked more like a large box than a ship.

    A - TRUE   B - FALSE

7. How old was Noah when the flood started?

    A - 950   B - 550   C - 600   D - 100

8. Where did the water for the flood come from?

    A - Rain clouds.
    B - A collapsing vapor, or water canopy.
    C - It didn't, because the flood is only a legend.
    D - The fountains of the deep.

9. The entire earth was covered by water.

    A - TRUE   B - FALSE

10. The rain fell on the earth for…

    A - 40 days and nights.
    B - 150 days and nights.
    C - 364 days and nights.
    D - 375 days and nights.

11. Animals only began to fear man after the flood.

      A - TRUE   B - FALSE

12. There is no real evidence today that there ever was a global flood.

      A - TRUE   B - FALSE

13. Fossils…

      A - are made over millions of years.
      B - cannot be found on the major mountains of the world.
      C - can be accurately dated using the "geological column".
      D - none of the above.
      E - all of the above.

14. Up until shortly after the flood, there was only one language in the world.

      A - TRUE   B - FALSE

Write the correct answer in the space provided:

15. After the flood, mankind was given permission to eat _____.

16. As a sign of His promise never to destroy the earth with water again, God placed a _____ in the sky.

17. Write down two evidences from the earth that indicate a water event at some time in the past.

      a. _____

      b. _____

18. The Tower of Babel was located on the Plain of _____.

19. What two things did God do at Babel?

      a. _____

      b. _____

20. Name 4 of the 5 important events that are included in the "creation model".

      a. _____

      b. _____

      c. _____

      d. _____

UNIT FOUR – TEST

Circle the letter of the correct answer for each of the following questions:

1. The word "science" means…

   A - experiments   B - evolution   C - knowledge   D - education

2. Evolution…

   A - must be accepted by faith..
   B - is an unproven theory.
   C - is religious in nature.
   D - is none of the above.
   E - is all of the above (A, B & C).

3. Major pillars, or steps, in evolution are…

   A - big bang
   B - life from non-life
   C - simple to complex
   D - none of the above
   E - all of the above (A, B, & C)

4. At each of these steps, scientists have been able to observe and demonstrate evolution theory.

   A - TRUE   B - FALSE

5. Three planets in our solar system do not spin the way evolution theory says they should.

   A - TRUE   B - FALSE

6. Each planet in our solar system…

   A - is unique.
   B - is made of the same quantities of elements.
   C - flew off of the sun billions of years ago.
   D - spins the same way as all the others.

7. Scientists have a theory, or perhaps several theories, about how stars form.

   A - TRUE   B - FALSE

8. Scientists know how stars form.

   A - TRUE   B - FALSE

9. Scientists have directly observed stars forming.

   A - TRUE   B - FALSE

137

10. Panspermia teaches that…

    A - life was created by God.
    B - flies and rats evolved from garbage.
    C - life came to the earth from somewhere in outer space.
    D - life becomes more complex.

11. Mutations have been observed to add complexity to living organisms.

    A - TRUE   B - FALSE

12. When scientists tests the age of rocks, their conclusions are always scientific.

    A - TRUE   B - FALSE

Write the correct answer in the space provided:

13. To try prove a theory, tests must be performed that are…

    a. _____

    b. _____

    c. _____

14. Biology is the study of _____

15. The special "code of life" that is present in all living things is called _____

16. According to evolution, the earth must be very _____ for evolution to have taken place.

UNIT FIVE - TEST

Circle the letter of the correct answer for each of the following questions:

1. According to evolution, mankind has been evolving from an ape creature for...

    A - 4½ billion years.
    B - 2 – 4 million years.
    C - 1 billion years.
    D - 16 billion years.

2. Creatures that appear on the "apes-to-man" chart are...

    A - all apes or humans.
    B - made up from fossil fragments.
    C - accepted as hominids by faith.
    D - all of the above.
    E - none of the above.

3. "Nebraska Man" and "Piltdown Man" are good examples of very bad science.

    A - TRUE   B - FALSE

4. There are no fossils that prove that humans evolved from ape-like creatures.

    A - TRUE   B - FALSE

5. Examples of "hominids" that turned out to be something quite different are...

    A - Piltdown Man
    B - Ramapithecus
    C - Cro-Magnon Man
    D - Nebraska Man
    E - all of the above.
    F - none of the above.

6. "Cro-Magnon Man" and "Neanderthal Man" are fully human.

    A - TRUE   B - FALSE

7. "Lucy" is a problem for her discoverer, Dr. Donald Johanson, because...

    A - most scientists say she's just an ape.
    B - the key bone Johanson said made her walk upright was found far away.
    C - she's the height and size of a chimpanzee – about 3½ feet.
    D - all of the above.
    E - none of the above.

8. Scientists know, from fossils, exactly what the creature would have looked like when it was alive.

    A - TRUE   B - FALSE

UNIT SIX - TEST

Circle the letter of the correct answer for each of the following questions:

1. According to Romans 1:20, what has been clearly seen?

    A - God's invisible qualities.
    B - All of the animals of the world.
    C - Evolution.
    D - The Gospel.

2. The Mallee fowl must...

    A - make a brand new nest every day.
    B - help their babies to crawl up through the dirt once they hatch.
    C - keep the eggs at an exact temperature, otherwise the chicks inside will die.
    D - all of the above.
    E - none of the above.

3. A butterfly learns from its parents where to find food.

    A - TRUE   B - FALSE

4. A giraffe's head is about 24 feet in the air.

    A - TRUE   B - FALSE

5. A giraffe has a very strong head to resist the blood pressure when it drinks.

    A - TRUE   B - FALSE

6. The honeyguide and the honey badger from Africa...

    A - are good examples of creatures that display a symbiotic relationship.
    B - know by instinct how to respond to each other.
    C - both need bees to stay alive.
    D - all of the above.
    E - none of the above.

7. The chameleon...

    A - can change color automatically.
    B - is often killed by Africans who fear that it has a demon living inside it.
    C - is not even aware that its color is changing.
    D - all of the above.
    E - none of the above.

8. Birds do not need to learn how to build nests; they know how by instinct.

    A - TRUE   B - FALSE

9. The bombardier beetle…

    A - drops bombs on picnickers.
    B - is a type of small, German car.
    C - has a cannon that can fire a hot, smelly substance.
    D - all of the above.
    E - none of the above.

10. Spiders have the ability to think about the things they do.

    A - TRUE   B - FALSE

Write the correct answer in the space provided:

11. According to Romans 1:20, God's invisible qualities are His _____

    and His _____.

12. Romans 1:20 says that people are without _____.

13. The Mallee fowl is found in what country? _____.

14. Most stinging insects are _____ compared to humans. It's a good thing, too!

15. Even though we cannot prove the existence of God by science, nature provides us with all the

    _____ we need to believe He exists.

UNIT SEVEN - TEST

Circle the letter of the correct answer for each of the following questions:

1. The word "dinosaur"…

    A - was first used by Job.
    B - was first used in 1940.
    C - is a word that only evolutionists use.
    D - means "terrible lizard".

2. Dinosaurs…

    A - ruled the earth during the Mesozoic period.
    B - died out about 65 million years ago.
    C - never really existed – they were just made up by the evolutionists .
    D - all of the above.
    E - none of the above.

3. The Iguanodon is considered to be the first dinosaur ever discovered.

    A - TRUE   B - FALSE

4. There are no fossils that show a reptile turning into a bird.

    A - TRUE   B - FALSE

5. The main difference between modern lizards and dinosaurs is that…

    A - dinosaurs ruled the earth at one time; modern lizards don't.
    B - dinosaurs all grew large; modern lizards don't.
    C - dinosaurs' legs were below the body; modern reptiles' legs grow out of the side of the body.
    D - all of the above.
    E - none of the above.

6. Reptiles never stop growing as long as they're alive.

    A - TRUE   B - FALSE

7. The very large dinosaurs might have been very old ones.

    A - TRUE   B - FALSE

8. The "geological column"…

    A - is an accurate "map" of the history of the earth.
    B - divides evolutionary time for the age of the earth into five basic periods.
    C - basically agrees with the Bible's version of the age of the earth.
    D - shows how evolution took place.

9. Noah possibly took baby animals onto the ark because baby animals…

      A - don't take up as much room as adults.
      B - eat less food than adults.
      C - won't fight with each other.
      D - all of the above.
      E - none of the above.

10. Evolutionists say that dinosaurs lived during the Mesozoic Period.

      A - TRUE   B - FALSE

Write the correct answer in the space provided:

11. A characteristic of a reptile is that there are generally _____ on the skin.

12. Reptiles cannot generate heat for their bodies from the food that they eat. Creatures like this are

    called _____.

13. The largest fossilized reptile eggs ever found are about _____ inches long.

14. The average size of a dinosaur was the size of a large _____.

15. On the "geological column", the term "Mesozoic" means _____.

16. The Bible genealogies indicate that the earth is about _____ years old.

17. There were 1,656 years between the creation and the _____.

18. _____ brought the animals to Noah to put on the ark.

19. According to the book of Job, the _____ was chief among "the works

    of God".

20. A _____ could make real fire come out of its mouth.

Index

Some Recommended Resources...

BOOKS & DVDs

In The Beginning, Dr. Walter Brown, CSC

Evolution: The Grand Experiment, Dr. Carl Werner, New Leaf Press *

The Complete Zoo Adventure, Mary & Gary Parker, Master Books *

A Closer Look at the Evidence, Richard & Tina Kleiss, Search for the Truth Ministries *

The Big Book of Animal Devotions, William Coleman, Bethany House *

Global Warming and the Creator's Plan, Jay Auxt & Dr. William Curtis III, Master Books

Dinosaur Activity Book, Earl & Bonita Snellenberger, Master Books *

The True Story of Noah's Ark, Tom Dooley & Bill Looney, Master Books *

Dinosaurs by Design, Duane T. Gish, Ph.D., Master Books *

What is Creation Science?, Morris/Parker, Master Books

The Evolution of a Creationist, Dr. Jobe Martin, Biblical Discipleship Publishers

Buried Alive, Dr. Jack Cuozzo, Master Books

The Revised Quote Book, Dr. Andrew Snelling, AIG

Bone of Contention, Sylvia Baker, Evangelical Press *

Unlocking the Mystery of Life, Illustra Media DVD

The Privileged Planet, Illustra Media DVD

The Return to Genesis; The Horror of the Flood; The Mystery of the Dinosaurs; The Pillars of Evolution; Aunt Lucy?; The Hunters and the Hunted; Lost Secrets of the Ancient Civilizations, Mike Snavely, Live Seminar Series, Mission Imperative Video Production *

Grand Canyon: The Puzzle on the Plateau, Mike Snavely, Mission Imperative Video Production

---

NOTE: The above list is by no means exhaustive. There are many other fine resources. This list will at least provide the student an excellent start for further study. (Resources marked with a * are not strictly geared for adults. Children can benefit from these as well.)

About the Author...

Mike Snavely was reared in South Africa, the son of missionary parents. His father was a bush pilot for a rural mission hospital among the Zulu people. Throughout his life he has been fascinated with wildlife. Growing up in an area that teemed with remarkable and diverse creatures, he had a wide variety of "pets" and fascinating experiences which helped to mold his future. After graduating from Oak Hills Christian College in Minnesota in 1979, he returned to South Africa to work for the National Parks Service in the world-famous Kruger National Park. In some circles, this has earned him the nickname, "Ranger Mike".

Following this, he began a career as an African wildlife artist. In 1985 he married Carrie Baum who grew up near Hershey, Pa. Carrie attended Lancaster Bible College and was an executive secretary for the Pa. Turnpike Commission before becoming a full-time mom. In 1986 they returned to South Africa with TEAM (The Evangelical Alliance Mission) and served by teaching at Durban Bible College. Since returning to the U.S. they have developed a ministry of teaching creation (vs. evolution) through a seriers of seminars, and using nature and wildlife as a basis. They established Mission: Imperative in

1995 as a 501(c)(3), not-for-profit corporation. The ministry necessitates much travel, both in this country and abroad. Mike and Carrie have home-educated their three children since 1991 --- Luke (1986), John (1989), and Laura (1991).

The "Creation Safari" seminars Mike has developed are not dry lectures, nor does he speak over people's heads. His approach is to make these sessions as interesting and understandable as possible so the information will be remembered. He uses PowerPoint, video, puppets and other props. The use of humor adds to the interest.

Mike is the author of Creation of Evolution: A Home-Study Curriculum and has, so far, produced eight DVDs on a wide range of topics relative to creation issues.

www.natureofcreation.org

147